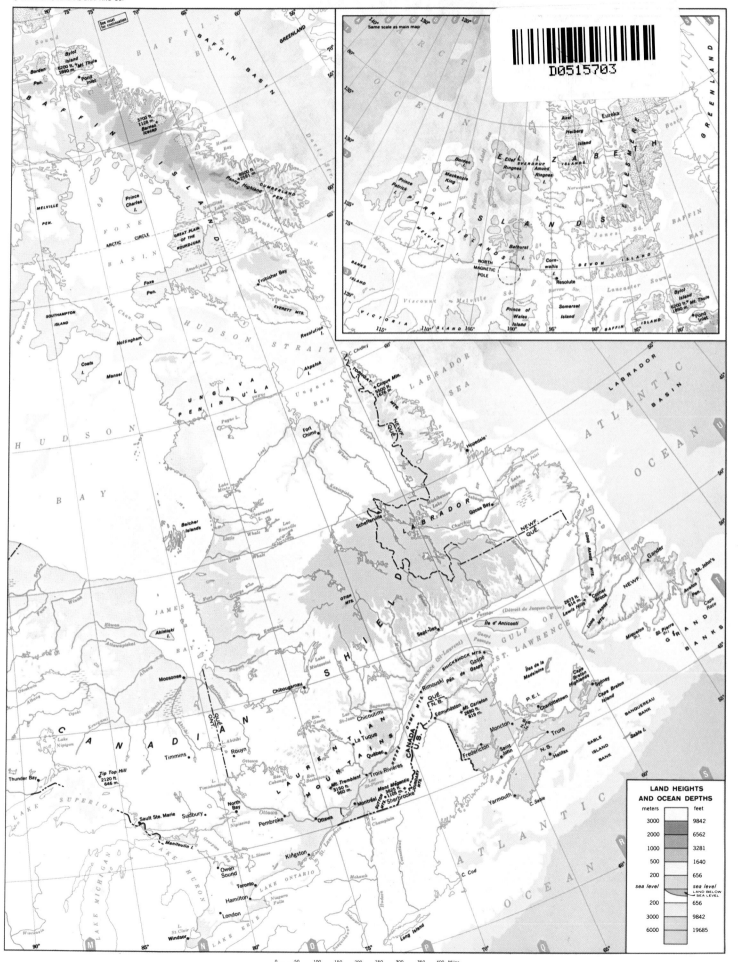

D0515703

LAND HEIGHTS AND OCEAN DEPTHS

meters		feet
3000		9842
2000		6562
1000		3281
500		1640
200		656
sea level		sea level
	LAND BELOW SEA LEVEL	
200		656
3000		9842
6000		19685

0	50	100	150	200	250	300	350	400 Miles

0	100	200	300	400	500	600 Kilometers

61289

Prince Edward Island

ANTHONY HOCKING

Publisher: John A. Savage

Managing Editor: Robin Brass

Manuscript Editor: Jocelyn Van Huyse

Production Supervisor: Rachel Mansfield

Graphics: Pirjo Selistemagi

Cover: Brian F. Reynolds

◧THE CANADA SERIES

McGRAW-HILL RYERSON LIMITED

Toronto   Montreal   New York   St. Louis   San Francisco
Auckland   Bogotá   Düsseldorf   Johannesburg
London   Madrid   Mexico   New Delhi   Panama
Paris   São Paulo   Singapore   Sydney   Tokyo

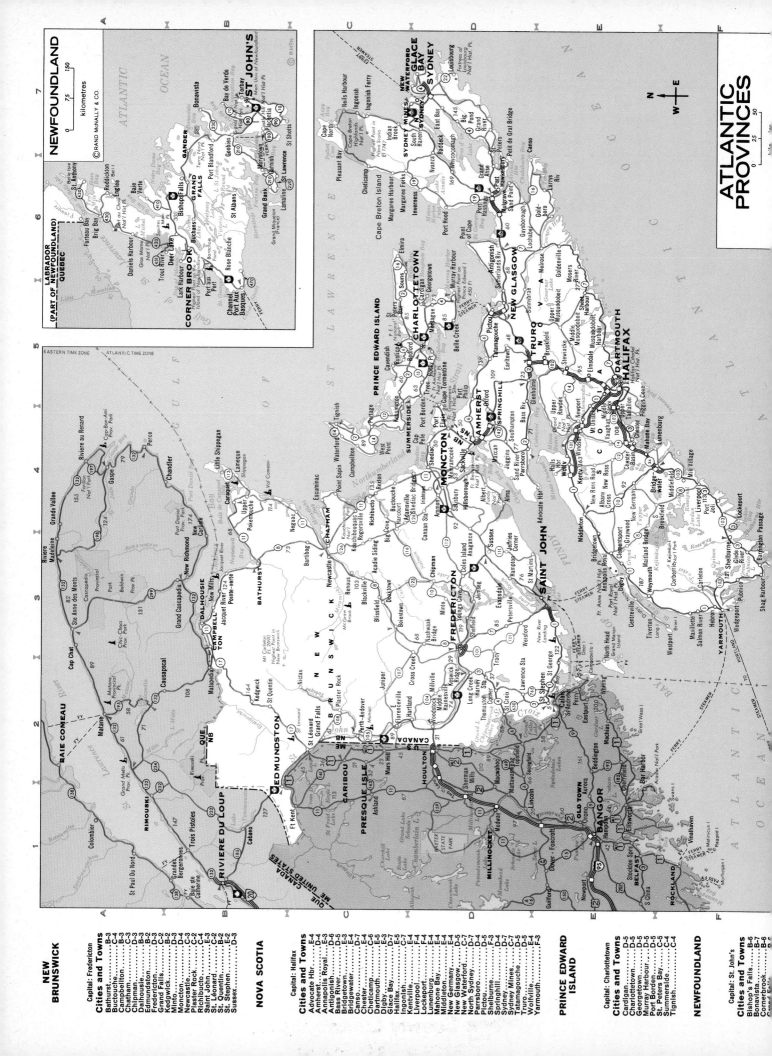

ATLANTIC PROVINCES

NEWFOUNDLAND

© RAND McNALLY & CO.

LABRADOR
(PART OF NEWFOUNDLAND)
QUEBEC

CORNER BROOK
GRAND FALLS
GANDER

ST. JOHN'S

NEW BRUNSWICK

PRINCE EDWARD ISLAND

CHARLOTTETOWN

NOVA SCOTIA

SYDNEY MINES
NORTH SYDNEY
GLACE BAY
NEW WATERFORD

NEW GLASGOW
TRURO
AMHERST
SPRINGHILL

DARTMOUTH
HALIFAX

SUMMERSIDE

MONCTON
FREDERICTON

SAINT JOHN

BATHURST
CHATHAM
NEWCASTLE

CAMPBELLTON
DALHOUSIE

EDMUNDSTON

YARMOUTH

BANGOR
OLD TOWN
PRESQUE ISLE
CARIBOU
MILLINOCKET
BELFAST
ROCKLAND

RIVIÈRE DU LOUP
BAIE COMEAU
RIMOUSKI

CONTENTS

PRINCE EDWARD ISLAND

Canada's smallest province has had many names. Micmac Indians called it '*Minagoo*,' simply 'the Island,' or more romantically '*Abegweit*,' meaning 'cradled on the waves.' The French knew it as 'Ile St. Jean,' which the English translated as 'St. John's Island.'

In the 1780s, confusion with St. John's in Newfoundland led settlers to rename the colony 'New Ireland' — a match for 'New Scotland' (Nova Scotia) on the mainland opposite, and 'New England' farther south. But the British Privy Council refused to sanction the change because another New Ireland already existed. Instead, the Island — spelled with a capital 'I' since the first days of English settlement — was eventually renamed after Prince Edward, Duke of Kent and commander-in-chief of the forces in British North America.

Prince Edward never set foot on his namesake, but in 1837 his daughter Victoria became its queen. Perhaps in Victoria's honour, Islanders allowed Prince Edward's name to remain on the map. They themselves, however, seldom referred to the colony as anything but 'the Island' — as opposed to everything 'away' on the mainland or beyond. The Island's surface area and population were small, but the inhabitants were self-sufficient.

In 1873 Prince Edward Island joined Canadian Confederation, and in the process gained equal legal status with much larger provinces. The Island proudly retains this status to the present, even though it amounts to only one-tenth of one per cent of Canada's land area, and holds barely one-half of one per cent of its population.

At various times outsiders have proposed political union of the Island and its mainland neighbours, New Brunswick and Nova Scotia. Islanders, however, stoutly resist the idea. They value their separate history and heritage, and see no compelling reason to abandon local self-government, which has served them well for more than two centuries.

Island fishermen catching lobsters off the north coast. Fresh lobsters are among the Island's great delicacies.

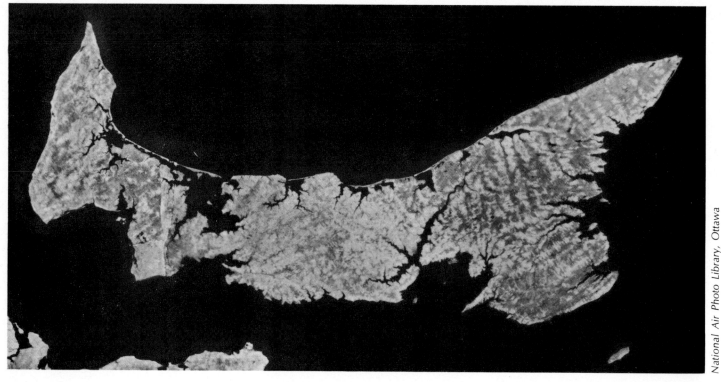

LAND AND SEA

The Gulf of St. Lawrence is studded with an entrancing assembly of islands, each a world of its own and magically different from its neighbours. Some are big like Anticosti, some are tiny like the Magdalens, but the gem of the collection is Prince Edward Island.

The Island originated in sediment drained into the gulf from surrounding mountain systems, notably the ancient rocks of the Canadian Shield. The action of wind and water through eons steadily wore down this rock, and sand — tinted red by the presence of iron oxide — was washed to the gulf's bottom. There the sand was deposited in layers over deep salt beds formed in an earlier period. The sediments were compacted by the weight of subsequent layers dumped above them, until eventually the distinctive red sandstone which makes up the Island and the neighbouring lowlands of eastern New Brunswick was formed.

The period of the Island's original formation occurred about 200 million years ago, during the Permian or perhaps the Carboniferous period. Much more recently, beginning about 100 000 years ago, the great Wisconsin glacier of the final Ice Age began its long march over most of North America. The Island lay in its path, and was submerged by it for long stretches of time

The Wisconsin's progress was erratic. Overall it moved on a north-south axis, but occasionally it slipped in an east-to-west direction, or vice versa, and each time exerted immense pressure on the rock far beneath its surface. Periodic advances and withdrawals climaxed about 25 000 years ago, when the Wisconsin's final retreat commenced.

While the glacier melted, it is possible that Northumberland Strait was much narrower than it is now. Certainly the sea was much lower, because so much of it was still frozen within the glacier. Gently sloping drainage valleys gouged out by the ice, which continue below present sea level, carried silt into Northumberland Strait and the Gulf of St. Lawrence off the Island's north and eastern shores.

The glacier had scraped soil and rock from the sedimentary formations beneath, and had pushed or rolled this debris to new locations. In western districts of the Island there are boulders of igneous origin which were apparently carried from eastern New Brunswick. But most of the debris is brown-red, sandy, stone-free soil which still cloaks the Island, acidic and low in plant nutrients, but unusually deep and with great potential for agriculture providing it is properly treated.

The soil cover has been increased through the effects of wind and water

A mosaic of ERTS satellite photographs shows the even terrain on the Island's north coast, facing the Gulf of St. Lawrence, which contrasts with the more rugged character of the west, south, and east shores.

on the soft sandstone, for the Island's geophysical evolution has never stopped. The result is a strikingly even terrain over most of the Island — gently rolling contours following the sedimentary layers beneath, and never high above sea level.

Only two areas are distinctly hilly — one in western Queens County, the other in southern Kings County. Here soils are thin and suffer from excessive drainage. Parts of western Prince county are swampy, and soils are poorly drained and unsuitable for agriculture. Even so, nearly 60 per cent of the Island is suitable for cultivation.

Soils apart, mineral resources are negligible. The only minerals currently exploited are structural materials like gravel and sand, and even they are in short supply. Traces of oil and natural gas have been found, and west of O'Leary there are indications of uranium, but it is unlikely that these deposits are extensive enough to be worth developing.

Topography

The Island is narrow and crescent-shaped — nearly 200 km from its eastern tip to its northern extremity, and between 6.5 km and 56 km across. No part of it is more than 16 km from the sea.

The coast is liberally indented by bays and tidal inlets. In the east and south some of these inlets provide fine harbours, and the best is at Charlottetown. On the north shore, however, sand dunes block the inlets and prevent all but small boats from using them as harbours.

Most Island rivers are really sea creeks, since the tides flow to their heads where they meet modest streams flowing from the interior. The streams wash eroded soil towards the sea. There are few ponds or lakes of any size, but the Island has many saltwater lagoons enclosed by dunes.

A patchwork of fields and farm woodlots carpets much of the Island. No part of it is more than 16 km from the coast.

The Island's coastline is frequently indented by deep bays and long tidal inlets, but here on the north shore troublesome sand dunes restrict the use of natural harbours to small boats.

Sandstone cliffs on the Island's south and east coasts are attacked by wind and wave action, and each year parts of them crumble into the sea.

THE ECOSYSTEM

To visitors, one of the Island's chief delights is its 'unspoiled' scenery — the well-kept farms and peaceful hamlets in the central core, the rougher terrain in the east and the west. But in reality the Island ecosystem is almost all artificial.

Islanders have been tampering with the natural environment since the early days, and long ago broke down the Island's natural forest cover to exploit its timber resources and to clear space for agriculture. By 1900 about 80 per cent of the Island forest had been cleared, and disease attacked what remained.

Since then, much of the 'farmland' has been abandoned and has returned to forest through the invasion of opportunist species, notably the white spruce. Very few examples of the original climax forest cover — mostly broad-leaved trees, with maple, birch, and oak predominant — have survived.

Apart from the few stands of native forest, the only authentic habitats remaining on the Island are its sand dunes and salt marshes. Both were utilized by early settlers, French and English — the grass-grown dunes as cattle pasture, the marshes for the cultivation of marsh hay to provide winter forage. But both were abandoned as settlers cleared the forest and moved inland.

The dunes are formed from sand washed ashore by wave action, then dried by the wind and blown on to the growing mound behind the beach. The sand is prevented from spreading farther by marram grass, a tall, long-rooted species that grows with the dune and holds it remarkably stable. The marram grass acts as a windbreak and allows other plants to take root in the dune — notably beach pea and bayberry. However, in cases where the marram grass is broken down — for instance, where it is trampled — sand may spread unchecked and inundate agricultural land or silt up fishing harbours.

The most impressive Island dunes are those of white sand on the north coast, but white dunes are found on the eastern and western coasts too. Only in the south are there red sandstone cliffs, which are so soft that each year parts of them tumble into the sea and in the process form more sand to be washed ashore in due course.

The Climate

At the Island's latitude, air masses tend to move eastward from the North American continent towards the Atlantic, and temperatures fluctuate more widely than is normal on an island. On the other hand, moist air from the sea tends to offset much of winter's cold and summer's heat.

The Island thus has a relatively temperate climate, which is one of the chief reasons for its success as an agricultural producer. Winters are long and fairly cold, springs slow and chilly, summers pleasantly cool, and autumns late and warm. At least 3½ months are

On the Island, fall comes late but it is warm and in some ways the most appealing of the seasons. Country lanes blaze with colour for many weeks.

frost-free, ample for successful root and forage crop production.

Compared with other parts of the Atlantic region, the Island is little troubled by fog and mist. However, ice floes form in early January and may cover up to 80 per cent of the Northumberland Strait and nearby gulf waters in February and March, depending on winter and spring temperatures.

Island winters are long but reasonably mild, and the landscape takes on new patterns as storms bring heavy snows from the west.

The second authentic habitat, salt marsh, is the result of periodic inundations of the sea at times of unusually high tides. In the intervals between tides, a bog remains and plants take root — notably two types of cord grass, which provided the 'marsh hay' favoured by early Acadians and later by English-speaking settlers. Salt marshes are located all over the Island, wherever salt-water rivers or bogs touch the coastline. Ironically this land, which was the first to be cultivated by both French and English-speaking settlers, was also the first to be abandoned. It was later dismissed as waste and therefore escaped development.

The authentic habitats account for only a small proportion of the Island's surface area when compared with the artificial environments. But the new habitats are interesting too. The original Island flora and fauna were not nearly as varied as those of the mainland, but the introduction of exotic species has made a great difference.

Some of the interlopers are far from beneficial — for instance, ragweed, traditionally associated with hay fever, and wild mustard — but others have added new beauty. One is the lupin, originally a garden flower but now found wild all over the Island. Several rose varieties are following suit.

At one stage it seemed that the Island flower, the Lady Slipper, was doomed because so many were being picked. Seeds were sprayed from the air over eastern Kings, a prime habitat of the flower, but the effort failed because the seeds did not take root. Fortunately, however, the Lady Slipper has made a comeback on its own.

Sand dunes are among the Island's few authentic habitats, prevented from spreading inland by marram grass rooted deep in the dunes. The grass acts as a windbreak and allows other plants to take root.

7

Long before the arrival of white men, Micmac Indians regularly visited the Island from the mainland on summer hunting trips and it is possible that some settled permanently. A Micmac encampment has been recreated at Rocky Point, near the site of Port La Joye.

Few traces of the original Acadian settlements of Ile St. Jean have survived. This Acadian gravestone marked only with a cross came from a cemetery in the Scotchfort region, in north-eastern Queens.

Under the French, a garrison was stationed at Port La Joye, renamed Fort Amherst when the British occupied the Island in 1758. The site of the old capital is a national historic park.

ILE ST. JEAN

The first written record of the Island was left by Jacques Cartier, who landed on its north-west tip in July 1534. Cartier failed to realize that it was not part of the mainland, and made no attempt to circumnavigate it. But his description was flattering.

'All this land is low and flat,' he wrote, 'the most delightful that may be seen, and full of beautiful trees and plains. . . . In a word there was nothing lacking but good harbours.' These he tried to locate, but decided that they were an impossibility because the land was so low and the shore was lined with sandbars and dunes.

Cartier and his men several times spotted Indians on the Island, especially in Malpeque Bay, which they named *Rivière des Barques* because of the Micmac canoes that they sighted there. They could not induce any of the Indians to parley, so they left presents on the beach and went on their way.

Cartier may not have been the first white man to land on the Island, for fishing fleets from Brittany, Normandy, and Northern Spain were active throughout the Gulf of St. Lawrence every summer. Certainly Micmacs were resident, at least during summer, since they were the successors of the more primitive 'Shellfish People' of an earlier era.

Not until the arrival of Samuel de Champlain early in the seventeenth century was the Island properly delineated. Champlain referred to an 'Ile St. Jean' in 1604 in one of a series of books he wrote about his journeys, entitled *Des Sauvages*, and the Island was portrayed adequately on his map of 1632. It is not clear why or at what stage the Island was named for St. John.

In 1650 *La Compagnie de la Nouvelle France*, founded to promote missionary activity and the fur trade in Canada, was granted new charters which included fishing rights in the Gulf of St. Lawrence and on the Atlantic coast, and rights to the land bordering those areas. An associate, Nicholas Denys, was appointed governor of this territory. Ile St. Jean was included in the grant, but Denys did nothing to encourage colonization. Only transient fishermen visited the Island.

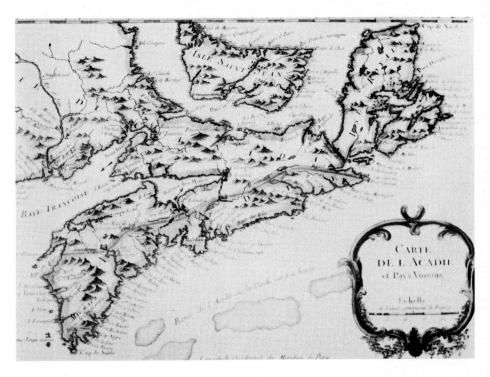

There was no deliberate settlement until 1710, when a number of Acadians settled there following the seizure of Port Royal and mainland Acadia (Nova Scotia) by New Englanders. The Acadians found that earlier that year a strip along the Island's southern coast had been granted as a seigneury to Louis de la Porte, Sieur de Louvigny, of Quebec. A few of them settled on marshland along the Hillsborough river, which they could drain and develop for agriculture, but most returned to the mainland.

In 1713 the Treaty of Utrecht confirmed Britain's possession of mainland Acadia, but ceded Ile St. Jean and Ile Royale (Cape Breton Island) to France. With the British so close, the two islands held special strategic significance for the French holdings on the St. Lawrence river, and France moved to strengthen them.

De Louvigny's grant of Ile St. Jean was rescinded by 1716, on the grounds that he had done nothing to develop his land. The Island and certain other islands in the Gulf of St. Lawrence were then granted to the Comte de Saint Pierre, a nobleman of the court of Louis XV, on condition that he introduced settlers.

A company was formed to finance Saint Pierre's scheme, and in 1720 three ships from France arrived in Hills-

Ile St. Jean was part of France's Acadia, and colonies were established at Port La Joye (the first Island capital, near what became Charlottetown), Saint Pierre (St. Peters Harbour), and Trois Rivières (near Brudenel on the east coast).

borough Bay carrying the first settlers. With the help of carpenters and other workers brought from Ile Royale, these settlers established the village of Port La Joye on a headland overlooking the sea.

Communities on the two islands were supposed to co-operate, but before long Saint Pierre found his trading efforts frustrated through keen competition from Ile Royale. He refused to pour more money into Ile St. Jean and allowed his company to go bankrupt. His grant was revoked in 1730, and his islands were reunited with the royal domain.

The next year a new grant was made, this time of only a part of the Island (the Brudenell region), to Jean Pierre de Roma. The new proprietor worked hard to introduce settlers and develop facilities, which came to include fisheries, a model farm, a forge, and other enterprises, and roads to other parts of the Island where settlers had established a foothold.

Walter Patterson was appointed governor of 'St. John's Island' in 1769. He remained in office until the British government dismissed him in 1786, on grounds of maladministration. In spite of his disgrace, most Islanders recognized that he had done more than anyone to make the colony a success.

As a result of Holland's survey of the Island, Charlottetown was developed as its capital. This watercolour by C. Randle depicts Charlottetown in 1778, during the American Revolution. After a privateers' raid on the town in 1775, a garrison was established there.

FRENCH AND ENGLISH

Stirred by French raids against remote settlements, a fleet from New England captured the great fortress of Louisbourg on Ile Royale in 1745. A contingent of New Englanders went on to seize De Roma's settlement on Ile St. Jean and also Port La Joye.

There had been a small French garrison at Port La Joye since 1724 — a contingent of twenty or thirty men — but it was powerless to resist the New Englanders. However, in 1748 the British government gave both Ile St. Jean and Ile Royale to France under the Treaty of Aix-la-Chapelle, in exchange for Madras in India. The New Englanders were not consulted.

From that year a steady stream of Acadians crossed to the Island from the mainland, where the British were demanding that they take an oath of loyalty to the British monarch. Unfortunately the new arrivals were an embarrassment, for there was not enough food. At the time, the Island was plagued annually by hundreds of thousands of fieldmice which destroyed all crops.

The stream of immigrants increased following the expulsion of the Acadians from Nova Scotia in 1755. But in 1758 Louisbourg fell to the British, and Ile St. Jean changed hands too. The British decided to transport Island Acadians to France. Some took to the woods, others escaped to Quebec, but the majority were deported.

Following this dispersal, no more than thirty French families remained on the Island, all that survived of more than 4000 Acadians. They stayed in hiding for several years, and were the ancestors of most of today's Island Acadians. Meanwhile, in 1763 Ile St. Jean and Ile Royale were annexed to Nova Scotia by proclamation of George III.

Persons of influence in Britain petitioned for grants of land on the 'Island of St. John' — nobody more fervently than the Earl of Egmont, who wanted all of it. However, the British authorities decided that the Island should first be surveyed and then divided into lots for redistribution among those whose claims were most pressing.

The survey was entrusted to Capt. Samuel Holland, surveyor-general of all British possessions in North America north of the Potomac river. He and his wife arrived in 1764 and set up headquarters in Port La Joye, now renamed Fort Amherst. Holland had been instructed to divide the Island into three counties, the counties into parishes, and the parishes into townships.

One of Holland's tasks was to select a town site in each county. He chose 'George Town' (named after George III) as county town of Kings in the east, 'Charlotte Town' (after King George's consort) for Queens in the centre, and 'Prince Town' (after the Prince of Wales) for Prince in the west. Each was surrounded by a 'royalty' of common land to provide pasture.

Holland tried to ensure that each

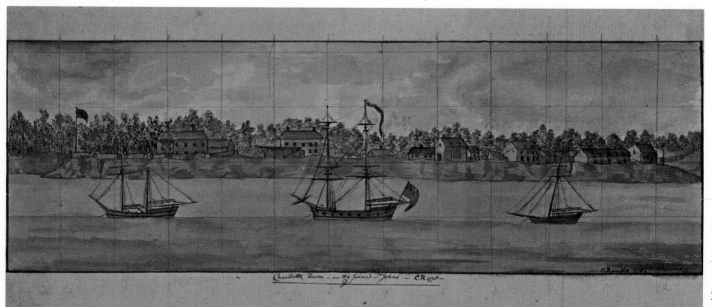

parish and township had access to the coast or to navigable rivers, as these were to be the highways. In all there were sixty-seven land lots, each of about 20 000 acres (8100 ha). Two were granted to the proprietors of existing fishing operations, and one was reserved for the Crown. The remainder were offered in a lottery.

Lots were drawn in July 1767, and deserving candidates were awarded land subject to a number of conditions. The most important of these required them to pay an annual quit-rent of between £20 and £60 beginning five years from the date of the grant, and to organize settlement of their township within ten years.

At the time of the draw, the Island was still part of Nova Scotia. In 1769, however, the new landowners (perhaps led by Walter Patterson) persuaded the home government that the Island should be a separate colony. They undertook to start paying quit-rent immediately if the home government agreed, which it did.

In 1769 Patterson was appointed captain-general and governor-in-chief of the Island. He landed there in 1770, and soon decided that the Island could become 'the garden of America' if his fellow-proprietors co-operated. However, very few troubled to send out settlers or to pay the required quit-rent. As a result, Patterson soon found that his administration was in financial difficulty. He set up the machinery of government, including the Island Supreme Court. Elections were held in 1772, and the Legislative Assembly first sat in 1773. The few settlers to arrive were small parties of Scots. Patterson established them on his own township, together with some displaced Acadians.

In 1775 Patterson sailed to Britain to report on Island affairs to the home government and the non-resident proprietors. He was supposed to be absent for only a year, but eventually stayed away for five.

Most Island Acadians were expelled in 1758, but at least thirty families survived undetected in the woods near Malpeque. An Acadian village has been developed at Mont Carmel in southern Prince to illustrate the Island's Acadian heritage.

The Privateers

While Governor Patterson was in Britain in 1775, two privateers from New England, supporting the rebel cause in colonies to the south, raided Charlottetown and made off with the settlement's winter supplies. The Americans also looted the houses of Patterson and Phillips Callbeck, the acting governor, seizing everything of value.

Callbeck and another official were carried off and deposited near George Washington's headquarters in Massachusetts, where they were treated courteously and released. The captains of the two privateers involved were relieved of their commissions. However, the plunder, including the Island's seal, was not returned.

As a result of the incident, the British despatched a sloop-of-war from Halifax to the Island, as well as four companies of soldiers to act as a garrison. But before they reached Charlottetown, the Malpeque area was raided by two more privateers, and so was St. Peters, where oxen and sheep were killed.

American privateers who raided Charlottetown in 1775 carried off senior officials and a quantity of booty, including the Island's great seal, which was never recovered. This replica bears the motif incorporated in the Island's coat of arms — three small oak trees, representing the Island's three counties, in the shade of a tall oak, representing British protection.

NEW SETTLERS

The American War of Independence ended in 1783, and large numbers of displaced Loyalists were transported to Nova Scotia in that year. Governor Patterson, in search of suitable settlers, persuaded a number of them to travel to the Island of St. John. Patterson intended to place the Loyalists on land confiscated from absentee landowners who had not paid the necessary quit-rents.

In 1774 the Island legislature had passed a law allowing the administration to auction off land on which quit-rents had not been paid, the proceeds going to the government. No effort had been made to implement the law until after Patterson's return from Britain in 1780. The next year a land auction had been arranged, but only government officials had been notified of its time and place. Patterson's idea had been that officials should be allowed to acquire confiscated land as compensation for salaries still unpaid.

On learning of this, affected landowners in Britain had appealed to the Colonial Office to annul the sales. Patterson had been ordered to return the land already sold, but he had refused. However, a serious quarrel with his chief justice, Peter Stewart, had led to a falling-out with Stewart's supporters, who formed a majority in the Assembly.

That was the situation in 1784, when Loyalist settlers arrived to take up land which Patterson had promised to them. They were obliged to spend the winter months in Charlottetown barracks, and many returned to Nova Scotia at the first opportunity. Others who remained soon found that their land title was by no means secure.

In 1785 Patterson himself was summoned to London by the Colonial Office to explain some of his actions. His replacement, Edmund Fanning, arrived late in 1786, but he found that Patterson was still in office and refused to leave. Some months later Patterson was formally dismissed. Even then he remained on the Island until 1789.

Fanning quickly allied himself with Stewart and his family, in a bid to outweigh Patterson's supporters. By

Charlottetown's pride is its natural harbour, which was the focus of Island trade during the nineteenth century. This view was painted by George Thresher in 1820, and shows the modest wharfing facilities then available.

1801 seven of a total of seventeen government officials (including judges) were members of the Stewart family. This was a 'Family Compact' even tighter than those in other colonies of British North America.

The Compact dominated the government, but was generally opposed by tenants of the countryside. Longest established of these were two parties of Scottish settlers that had arrived in 1770: one from Perthshire, about 200 colonists who had settled around Covehead in northern Queens, and the other from Argyllshire, settlers brought out by the Stewart family and settled around Malpeque.

Another settlement was New London, founded by the Quaker Robert Clark as a haven for members of his denomination persecuted by the

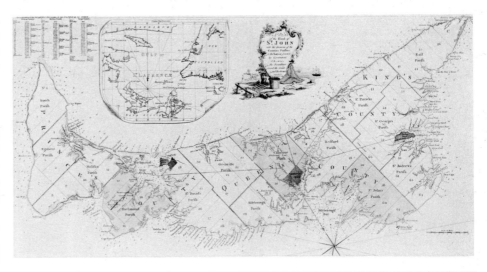

Church of England. But the biggest was Scotchfort near Tracadie, settled by more than 200 Scottish Catholics escaping Presbyterian evangelistic zeal in the Hebrides. They had reached the Island in 1772.

The Scotchfort pioneers were better organized than most. Their sponsor, John MacDonald of Glenaladale, had heard about the Island from Fraser Highlanders who had visited it following the capture of Quebec in 1759. He had sent out workmen in 1771, so a number of simple cabins were ready for his settlers when they arrived.

In contrast, most new arrivals were thrown on their own resources first to build a log cabin near a watercourse, and then to clear their land of trees. Only when this was done and the trees were burned could they plant potatoes and other crops, using the ash from the burned trees as fertilizer.

Immigration to the Island waned following the conclusion of the American War, and indeed many settlers left. Then in 1803 a party of 800 Scots arrived, most of them on board the *Polly*, and nearly all of them evicted crofters who were victims of changing social conditions in the Scottish Highlands and the Hebrides. Their move to North America was organized by Lord Selkirk, who had visions of opening the New World to mass colonization. Most of the Selkirk settlers were granted land in what became Belfast.

Temporarily frustrated in efforts to acquire land for settlement in the west, Selkirk had bought large tracts of Island land on which quit-rent was owing. His settlers, many of them from the Isle of Skye, first established themselves in improvised wigwams of poles interlaced with foliage. Selkirk's original estates were in south-eastern Queens, but he extended his holdings and acquired land in Prince and central Queens too. By 1814 he and John Cambridge, another absentee landlord with large holdings, owned sixteen of the Island's sixty-seven land lots between them.

Agriculture

Early settlers quickly cleared land of trees, burned the slash, and planted potatoes among the stumps. As stumps rotted they were pulled out and burned, and the settlers ploughed their land in readiness for more ambitious crops, particularly feed for livestock.

Grain was scattered by hand, and harvested with scythes or sickles. It was gathered with wooden rakes, threshed with flails on earthen or wooden threshing floors, and tossed into the air so that the chaff would blow away. Not until 1828 was the first threshing machine introduced, and the first mechanical reaper was imported in 1830.

Island soil was naturally acidic, and to counteract this condition farmers covered fields with alluvial mud rich in mussels and other shellfish. The mud was excavated from the bottoms of salt creeks, and hauled to the fields by horse-drawn sleighs. There, spring ploughing crushed the shells and produced lime for the land. Some farmers gathered lobster or oyster shells washed up during storms and spread those instead. It is still possible to find shellfish remains in fields far inland.

From an early stage Islanders exported livestock, grain, and potatoes to Newfoundland, the Miramichi in New Brunswick, and Halifax in Nova Scotia. Their efforts were encouraged and assisted by Col. John Ready, lieutenant-governor from 1824 to 1831, who introduced many new techniques from Britain and imported registered livestock to upgrade Island cattle.

Ready regularly visited all parts of the Island to learn of settlers' problems, and helped to establish a series of agricultural associations. During his period in office, Island agriculture achieved the prominence that it has never since relinquished.

Island soil is naturally acidic and not especially fertile. To improve it, farmers dug alluvial mud from saltwater creeks during winter and hauled it to their land by sled.

Ice racing, forerunner of today's harness racing, was popular on the Island in the nineteenth century. Weather permitting, weekly races are still held throughout winter on the ice of North river causeway in Charlottetown. Owners race second-grade horses rather than the first-grade animals which appear at the major driving parks.

Coles   Cooper

William Cooper, founder of the Escheat Party, and George Coles, leader of the Reform Party, dominated Island politics in the 1840s and the 1850s. Their efforts led to organized protest by tenants demanding escheat of estates owned by absentee proprietors.

Charlottetown's market square in 1873, as painted by Mrs. W. H. Bayfield. The rotunda and other buildings were destroyed in a serious fire in 1866. This is a contemporary copy by an unknown artist. The rotunda stood on the site of today's Confederation Centre of the Arts.

THE LAND QUESTION

Island landlords were represented by land agents who arranged leases for tenants and collected rents. These agents were supposed to evict tenants who fell behind with rent, but opposition to them was so intense that probably not even half of the rent was paid.

Tenants, whether original settlers or later arrivals, were indignant that they were not granted freehold of land they had developed, as was happening in other colonies of British North America. In fact, not only had they to pay rent, but they were also obliged to spend several days each year building and maintaining roads.

Their grievances surfaced in demands that the Island government should 'escheat,' or confiscate, land for which proprietors had not paid quit-rent (as had happened in Nova Scotia), and offer freehold to the tenants concerned. The tenants' rights were championed by a new political organization, the Society of Loyal Electors. In 1803, several members of the society were returned to the Assembly.

In 1819 one of the landlord's agents, Edward Abell, was shot and killed by a tenant who was then helped to evade capture. Abell was succeeded as land agent by William Cooper, a new arrival on the Island. Cooper proved efficient at his job, but within a few years he changed sides. In 1831 he ran for election to the Assembly on a platform of farmers' rights, and once elected he soon demanded a 'court of escheat' to settle the land issue.

Cooper now founded an 'Escheat Party,' which steadily increased its membership in the Assembly until in 1838 it won a majority. However, the measures it proposed were systematically blocked by the Family Compact or by the Colonial Office in London. Support for the idea of escheat waned, as more moderate Islanders decided that it was impractical and unfair to landlords who had purchased their title in good faith.

The Escheaters were defeated in 1842, and Cooper and others temporarily abandoned their cause. Meanwhile, tenants in Kings had been taking matters into their own hands, and where

Confederation Centre Art Gallery

possible banded together to oppose land agents. The county had become an unofficial 'liberated area' over which Charlottetown had little control.

On the Island, the coming power was the Reform Party of George Coles, who had formerly been associated with the Compact but had turned against it. Coles was joined by many former Escheaters who hoped to gain responsible government for the Island — an administration answerable to the Island legislature, unlike the Compact which was answerable only to the British government.

In 1850, Coles' supporters renamed themselves the Liberal Party. Their opponents, loyal to the Compact, were the forerunners of today's Conservative Party. In that year the Liberals were elected to power in the legislature, and in 1851 the British government agreed to their demands for responsible government.

In 1853 the Liberals passed the Land Purchase Act. This allowed the administration to purchase the land of proprietors willing to part with it, then re-sell to the tenants living on it. The first purchase under this act was made in 1854, but to effect it the administration had to use all the funds then available.

The new law did not go far enough to suit many tenants, and the 'liberated areas' in which no rent was paid swiftly increased. Not only Kings, but also much of northern Queens, was involved. Tenants warned each other of the approach of land agents and special constables by blowing on West Indian conch shells, long used by fishermen as foghorns.

By 1859 the Island government was in a position to purchase the Selkirk estates, and as before, land was sold to the former tenants. But progress was painfully slow. At the Island's request, the British government appointed a land commission to investigate conditions on the Island and make recommendations. One of its three members was Joseph Howe of Nova Scotia.

The commission rejected the idea of escheat, but did insist that all tenants should have the right to buy the land they occupied at a fair evaluation. It also suggested that the British government should guarantee a loan of £100 000, which would enable the Island administration to buy out the remaining landlords. The Island legislature prepared to implement the proposals, but its measures were vetoed by the British government.

Since the days of early settlement the Island's population has been predominantly rural, and more land was cleared for agriculture than is farmed today. Most of the agitation against absentee landlords took place in Kings and northern Queens. This watercolour, Landscape with Man and Cart, was painted c. 1880 by William C. Harris, brother of Robert Harris.

In response to this decision, tenants in all regions combined to form the 'Island Tenants' League,' pledged to withhold all rent until landlords agreed to sell on fair terms. A series of lively meetings reached a climax in 1865 when angry tenants marched on Charlottetown and demonstrated outside the Assembly.

A force of militia was sent to arrest one of the ringleaders, but was outwitted by Tenant Leaguers. They first halted the force before a 'fort' consisting of stove pipe 'cannon,' then allowed it to seize a straw-filled effigy of the man sought. Soon afterwards, however, professional troops sent from Halifax marched in to restore order. By the year's end, the tenants' revolt had been subdued.

CONFEDERATION

The Island had been granted responsible government in 1851, with George Coles as its first premier. The move had satisfied Islanders' political goals, and from that time the government concentrated on improving the Island's economic situation.

The economy received a major boost in the years following 1854, when Britain and the United States signed a reciprocity treaty permitting free trade between the Americans and the colonies of British North America. For some time Island farmers had indulged in 'unofficial' trade with American ships, but now it was legal.

Agricultural produce was the most important export, particularly during the years of the American Civil War. In 1859 the government had bought the great Selkirk estates under the Land Purchase Act, and the new freeholders made a major contribution. In Charlottetown a new class of Island merchants worked hard and prospered.

On the mainland, however, talk was of union. Upper and Lower Canada (Ontario and Quebec) were already united, and had been seeking closer ties with the other British colonies. This

was partly to promote their own trade, and partly to develop a common defensive network against possible attack from the United States.

Now Nova Scotia took the initiative, and in 1863 approached New Brunswick and the Island with proposals for a Maritime union. Island politicians could see no point in it unless such a union could provide money to buy more land from absentee proprietors. But the other Maritime colonies had no funds to spare.

Nova Scotia's plans were languishing when the Canadas intervened. They asked permission to send observers to any conference on Maritime union that might be held. The move prompted the Nova Scotians to try again. Realizing that the Island government was their biggest obstacle, they suggested that a conference should be held in Charlottetown.

Island politicians agreed — some of them hopeful that the capital of any union of colonies would be on the Island. But they insisted that delegates should merely discuss the possible advantages of union, not implement any definite plan. Parties from Nova Scotia, New Brunswick, and the Canadas arrived in Charlottetown on separate

steamers, in time for September 1, 1864.

Charlottetown was full — not, however, because of the conference, but because a circus from the mainland was in town. Little accommodation was available, and several delegates from the Canadas had to sleep on their steamer. Island leaders showed themselves aloof from mainland concerns, not convinced that there was any point in the negotiations.

The conference was held in the Colonial Building, today's Province House, in the Council's chamber. First, delegates from the Maritime colonies met to discuss matters of common concern. Later, the delegates from the Canadas were invited to explain their proposals for union of all British North America.

The Canadians laid heavy stress on the economic advantages of union. For the Island, these amounted to a plan to make available £200 000 to buy out the landlords. This assurance quickly changed Island delegates' views on the conference. One of the Canadians recorded that union of the provinces was unofficially proclaimed at a party that night, on board the steamer *Queen Victoria* in Charlottetown harbour.

Delegates remained in Charlottetown until September 10, when they adjourned to Halifax. There it was decided to hold a Confederation conference in Quebec City in October, where actual details on the union could be thrashed out. In Quebec, however, it became clear that the Canadians would not, after all, approve funds to buy Island land. With that, many of the Island representatives lost interest in Confederation, as did the bulk of the Island population. The British North America Act was passed in 1867, but the Island played no further part in negotiations and was not affected by it. Then in 1869 the new Dominion government offered 'improved terms' to the

The Charlottetown conference met in the council chamber of the Colonial Building, today's Province House. The conference table and chairs have been preserved, and plaques on the table mark the places occupied by delegates to the conference.

Voting in an Island election, as drawn in Charlottetown by Robert Harris c. 1880. Elections provided great entertainment for all sections of the community.

Island if it agreed to join Confederation.

Yet opposition continued. Island trade had slumped following the end of reciprocal trade with the United States in 1866, but in 1868 Americans themselves raised Island hopes. A delegation from Washington visited Charlottetown to propose a trade agreement between the Island and the republic — an idea so grand that not a few Island heads were turned.

In the event, the British government forced the Island to back off. Various economic sanctions were applied, apparently designed to shepherd the Island into Confederation. Islanders remained unconvinced until ensnared by debts arising from railway construction. Then, turning to the new Dominion government for help, the Island agreed to join Confederation on July 1, 1873.

By the 1870s, Summerside was a thriving community, profiting from its position opposite Shediac on New Brunswick's east coast. Shediac was connected with Moncton by railway, and therefore with the rest of Canada.

Delegates to the Charlottetown conference of 1864 posed for a photograph on the steps of Government House. John A. Macdonald of Canada West sits on the steps; George-Etienne Cartier of Canada East stands to his right; Charles Tupper of Nova Scotia is in the back row, second from the left; and Leonard Tilley of New Brunswick stands in front of the second pillar from the right. Island delegates included John Hamilton Gray, chairman of the conference, who stands at Macdonald's left; William Pope, back row, second from right; and George Coles, in front of Pope.

ISLAND PROVINCE

Under the terms of Confederation, the Island government could borrow up to $800 000 from the new Dominion government to buy land still held by absentee landlords. The Island's Land Purchase Act of 1875 obliged proprietors to sell their land at prices determined by a government commission.

About half of the land still held by proprietors was purchased within a year of the passing of the act. The remainder became the subject of court actions, as proprietors battled for their rights. Not

The one-room school was in many respects the focus of community life in most parts of the Island. This example, The School at Canoe Cove, on the Queens south coast, was painted by Robert Harris c. 1870.

Confederation Centre Art Gallery

Co-operation

From the early days, Islanders had felt a need for neighbourliness and co-operation. This was especially true when there was heavy work to be done, for instance land-clearing, barn-raising, ploughing, or harvesting with scythe and rake.

Typically, Islanders turned these exertions into 'frolics,' working through the day in expectation of a fine supper and probably a barn-dance through the

The Farmers' Bank of Rustico, founded in 1864, was the spiritual ancestor of all North America's credit unions, even though it was the smallest bank in Canada's history. It was eventually put out of business by a special act of the Dominion parliament.

night. While the men laboured in the open, the women usually organized a wool-carding or rug-hooking 'bee' indoors, at which all could hear the others' news and advice was freely exchanged.

Such bees and frolics symbolized the close relationship between social and economic activity on the Island — not unlike pioneer experience in many other parts of North America. On the Island, however, this informal co-operation was taken further, and its commercial possibilities were explored.

It was an Acadian community that led the way. In 1864 the priest of Rustico, George-Antoine Belcourt, helped local farmers to organize a tiny 'people's bank,' which was duly chartered by the Crown. To join it, each farmer bought one share, and the shareholders elected a board of directors from their own ranks. The bank lent money at interest rates far lower

than those otherwise available, and paid generous dividends. It never held assets of more than $4000 at one time, but it survived for thirty years before it was put out of business by a special act of the Dominion parliament. Alphonse Desjardins of Quebec later adopted the idea of the Farmers' Bank of Rustico in establishing his first *caisse populaire* in 1901, forerunner of all the credit unions of North America.

It was also Acadian farmers who organized the many grain co-operatives that flourished on the Island from the 1870s to the 1920s. Every Acadian parish had at least one. Farmers joined the grain bank by 'investing' a surplus of seed grain, and were eventually rewarded with modest dividends, also paid in grain. The banks lent seed to farmers at seeding time, and following the harvest expected 'a bushel and a peck' for each bushel borrowed — an interest of 25 per cent.

The grain banks were soon joined by a number of agricultural co-operatives involved in milk, egg, sheep, or potato production, or in shipping members' produce to outside markets. Eventually these co-operatives outlived their usefulness and were superseded by the marketing boards that operate today.

until 1893 was the last action settled. In each case the tenants resident on the appropriated land were given first option to buy it from the government.

In all, the Island borrowed $782 402.33 from the Dominion government, and has never repaid the sum, though it gained $600 000 from the sale of land to tenants. On the other hand, the Island did pay interest on the loan, a sum deducted from an annual subsidy of $45 000 paid by the Dominion government to compensate the Island for its lack of Crown lands.

As if in response to the settling of the land question, there was a marked upswing in agricultural productivity during the 1870s and 1880s. Farmers sold their produce to merchants in Charlottetown and Summerside, who shipped it to the mainland for transport to the markets of Central Canada.

At the same time, there was rapid growth in the Island fishing industry. The reciprocity treaty with the United States had ended in 1886, and American fishermen left Island waters. For the first time, Islanders in substantial numbers fished there instead, offering their catch to a number of modest canning plants which had appeared along the coasts. Between 1870 and 1880 the number of Island fishermen trebled, and the number of vessels involved more than doubled.

Agriculture and fishing provided adequate livelihoods for a great many Islanders, but they had limits. All land that had any agricultural potential was being farmed — getting on for 80 per cent of the Island's surface area, compared with less than 50 per cent farmed today. Farmers often had large families, and there was not enough land to go around.

Earlier, much of the surplus manpower had been absorbed in a multitude of small local industries serving the various local communities — mills, smithies, shoemakers, furniture makers, and many others. Before Confederation, such enterprises had been protected by a local tariff designed to make imports prohibitively expensive. In 1873, however, that tariff had been dropped as the Island threw in its lot with the other provinces.

At first, it was anticipated that sophisticated manufacturing industries would be established in all provinces, including the Island. Each of the Maritime provinces had developed a strong shipbuilding industry, and in New Brunswick, Saint John had already flowered as a significant manufacturing centre.

Perhaps with that example in mind, the Island raised no objections when the Dominion government introduced its 'national policy' in 1878. The national policy was expected to encourage industrial growth through immigration and railway development, and through protective tariffs which would allow Canadian industries to establish themselves.

Gradually it became clear that the national policy favoured Central Canada at the expense of the Maritimes — so much so that Island merchants were soon importing manufactured goods from the mainland for much less than Island enterprises could produce them. Inevitably the local industries swiftly declined, and were of no help in absorbing the surplus population emerging from the farms.

Throughout the nineteenth century steady immigration, particularly from Britain, and Islanders' natural increase boosted the population. From about 1880, however, the growth levelled off. In considerable numbers, younger Islanders were giving up hope of finding lucrative employment at home, and were heading for the booming cities of Central Canada or for the states of New England.

During winter the Island was cut off from the mainland by pack ice blocking Northumberland Strait. Convoys of ice boats made the crossing to the mainland, where possible sailed or rowed, but when necessary man-handled. Before agreeing to join Confederation, the Island insisted that regular steamer service be introduced to link the Island with the mainland in all seasons.

Public Archives of Canada, C30280

During the middle decades of the nineteenth century, shipyards were to be found on sheltered bays and creeks all around the Island, sometimes run in conjunction with other operations. Shown here are the residence, store, shipyard, and mills of the McLure Brothers of Murray River in Lot 63, a lithograph that appeared in J. H. Meacham's *Illustrated Historical Atlas of Prince Edward Island*, 1880.

Shipbuilders first laid a vessel's keel, and to it fastened the stem, sternpost, and frames. Here shipwrights lay the keelson above the frames over the keel, to provide longitudinal strengthening.

SHIPS AND FOXES

Until the 1830s, most Islanders subsisted through farming and perhaps fishing, with only limited prospects of trade with the merchants of Charlottetown and the world outside. Two industrial booms dramatically changed the situation.

The first was shipbuilding. The rich stands of hardwoods and softwoods pressing the shores of every creek and inlet were an open invitation to shipwrights, and as early as 1721 Saint Pierre's colonists had built three ships — one to carry salted cod to Europe,

one to hunt seals and sea cows in the Gulf of St. Lawrence, and one to trade with the West Indies.

Several small vessels were built in the early years of British settlement, but the industry's real beginnings came with the Treaty of Tilsit in 1807. Under the treaty, Scandinavian and Baltic nations were barred from supplying timber to Britain, which immediately turned to its colonies in North America. Enterprising merchants planned the export of Island timber to Halifax and Britain, and brought in skilled shipwrights to construct ships to transport it.

Between 1815 and 1840 several hundred ships were constructed on the Island. Many of them carried one cargo of Island timber to Britain and were then sold. Between 1840 and 1870 the Island shared in the shipbuilding boom experienced in all parts of the Maritimes and in Quebec too. Nearly 2500 ships were launched by Island yards, and sailed all over the world.

Shipyards were to be found at countless points along the Island's coasts. At their simplest they included only ways (the launching ramp), sawpits, a steam-box, a smithy, and probably sheds to shelter materials and tools, but some yards were much more sophisticated. Many Islanders learned specialized trades from the shipwrights brought in from outside, notably those from England's West Country, and they passed on their knowledge to Islanders who followed them.

In the early days Island timber was in plentiful supply. Hardwoods, like birch and juniper, were used for the keel and other sections below the waterline; softwoods, like spruce, were used for the remainder of the hull; and pine was used for masts. Gradually, however, supplies were depleted, and builders constructed whole vessels from spruce. Ultimately, much of the wood used in Island ships was imported from New Brunswick.

A high proportion of Island ships was sold to shipping interests in other countries, especially Britain. By the 1870s and 1880s, however, British shipowners turned increasingly to steam power and iron construction. Island merchants built ships for their own operations, but in the international market they found it difficult to compete with the larger, swifter windjammers built elsewhere. One by one, Island yards closed. As if in compensation, a quite different industry arose to fill the gap.

The new industry came about almost by accident. A young trapper and fur dealer, Charles Dalton of Tignish, became interested in the special properties of silver-black foxes, a rare mutant strain of the common red fox. Silver-black mutants brought much higher prices than conventional fox fur, and Dalton occasionally bought silver furs from Indians.

From 1880, Dalton set out to breed silver-black foxes. He acquired live animals from Indians, but not until 1887 did he produce a full litter of silver pups, and even then they died before reaching maturity. In 1890 Dalton joined forces with Robert Oulton of Alberton, and together they established a secret ranch on a tiny island. Oulton nursed a litter to maturity, and developed the principles of fox ranching.

At first Dalton and Oulton maintained their secrecy, but they were induced to sell breeding pairs to other residents of the Tignish-Alberton region. Several new fox ranches were established, and their combined production launched a new fashion craze in North America and Europe, but most of all in Russia. By agreeing not to sell live animals, the 'Big Six' fox ranchers of Tignish-Alberton operated as a cartel that controlled the international market.

In 1910 a member of the cartel sold breeding stock to a nephew of his in Summerside. The nephew was prepared to sell live animals for $10 000 a pair. He found many takers, and the industry boomed both on the Island and outside. By 1913 the Island held no fewer than 277 fox ranches, scattered in all regions.

With the outbreak of World War I, the exorbitant price of silver fox rapidly declined. Even so, Island fox farmers continued to make comfortable livings until the late 1930s. They were finally put out of business by the outbreak of World War II and the rise in popularity of short-hair furs like mink and muskrat.

The silver-black fox was the basis of an industry which made many Island fortunes before its collapse in the 1930s. The most important fox farms were located in western Prince.

THE ECONOMY

In the first twenty years following Confederation, the Island prospered. As before, its economy rested on agriculture, the fisheries, and local manufacturing, including shipbuilding. The population steadily increased, and small industries thrived.

From the mid-1890s until World War I, however, this progress was reversed. The Island's old markets declined, and the Island itself became a market for the produce of Central Canada, where rapid industrialization had taken place. During World War I the position briefly improved, but after the war came a slump during which the entire Maritime region lost its self-sufficiency.

As Central Canada's fortunes rose with those of the rest of North America, the Island and the other Maritime provinces marked time. The gap widened during World War II and immediately afterwards, as the central provinces profited from large capital expenditures by the federal government to increase industrial capacity.

Of course, many Islanders reacted to the growth elsewhere in Canada and in the United States by uprooting themselves and going to work there. Those who remained at home had little idea that they were worse off. Some remained in ignorance until the arrival of television during the 1950s, which roused sudden awareness of the material progress 'outside.'

A series of pioneer schemes followed, which were designed to improve economic conditions on the Island, culminating in the signing of Canada's first 'comprehensive development plan' between the federal and the provincial governments. Signed in 1969, the plan made provision for economic, social, and environmental programs over fifteen years. On the federal side, the plan involved the Department of Regional Economic Expansion (DREE), which had charge of the considerable funds available for approved projects. For the Island, a provincial Department of Development was created to co-ordinate the many programs, which could otherwise have conflicted or overlapped.

The plan is broadly the equivalent of the ten-year 'general development agreements' which DREE has signed with the other nine provinces. These agreements are broad statements of policy, under which specific programs are adopted as sub-agreements. The Island's plan, however, allows for ongoing programs in eighteen different spheres.

Some of these spheres directly involve primary industry, notably agriculture and fishing; others are concerned with manufacturing — particularly the assistance of small industry — and construction, which comprise the secondary sector of the economy; other spheres cover programs designed to boost tourism, assist commerce, and develop markets.

Social programs include the construction of new schools across the Island, vocational and employment training, housing assistance, and leadership training. Environmental programs have included the introduction of sewage treatment facilities, industrial waste disposal, and the monitoring of potential soil and water pollution.

The plan's original purpose was to increase employment opportunities and productivity on the Island to the point where it could stand on its own feet without relying on equalization payments from the federal government. Unfortunately, economic frustrations during the 1970s complicated the Island's position. Much of the plan's success was offset by unforeseen developments elsewhere in Canada and the world. Even so, the plan opened up many possibilities which had not been considered earlier, and for that alone the plan has been worthwhile.

High-power tuna fishing boats have become a common sight off the island's north-east coast. Sometimes the chase continues long after sunset.

Strawberries and blueberries grow well on the Island, adding variety to an agricultural industry famous for potatoes and dairy products.

A cheese factory in Summerside. The Island produces a surplus for export to the mainland.

Natural Resources

For more than a century the Island has relied on three principal assets — soil, sea, and scenery. In spite of new economic programs introduced under the comprehensive development plan, they will not quickly be replaced as the economy's chief supports.

Some say that the Island's agricultural belt is the finest in Canada east of the Niagara Peninsula. The soil is not especially rich or fertile, but in most areas it is deep and consistent, and with careful management it can produce fine crops.

The Island fishery has rapidly shrunk in importance in recent years, compared with its former pre-eminence. It has been outstripped by tourism, construction, and manufacturing, including the fish processing industry. But programs designed to improve matters have been introduced.

Scenery has always been the Island's special pride, and has long enchanted visitors. Mass tourism, however, is a relatively recent phenomenon. It takes place during a short season in summer and leaves the Island little affected.

Other natural resources are few. Forestry is limited, though it will increase. Mineral exploitation is confined to excavation of structural materials. The one sector capable of considerable expansion is light industry, catering to markets on the Island and outside, and utilizing the Island's human resources.

The Island's prime assets are soil, sea, and scenery famous for dazzling colour contrasts.

FARMING

Many Canadians know the Island as 'the million acre farm,' though actually its area is closer to 1.4 million acres (567 000 ha), and slightly less than half is under cultivation, Even so, that is a larger proportion than in any other province.

In earlier days as much as 80 per cent of the Island was cleared for cultivation, but much land has since been abandoned as unproductive or too remote from markets. The lapsed farmland had been cleared by hand and horsepower, and its relatively rough terrain has deterred farmers from introducing sophisticated machinery.

Besides, the whole pattern of Island farming has changed. In earlier days a farmer and his family kept some animals, grew hay and pasture to support them, raised such crops as grain and

potatoes to supplement their income, and probably also drew on the farm woodlot. Crop rotation and the spreading of manure helped to enliven the soil.

This was the pattern of Island farming until after World War II. Farmers prospered, and were encouraged to invest in new equipment and to embark on specialist enterprises like their counterparts across Canada. On the Island, the advantages of this policy had been demonstrated by fox farmers and by horse breeders catering to mainland forest industries.

During the 1950s, the Island government urged farmers to grow more potatoes. Earlier, farmers had raised potatoes in particular fields perhaps once every five years, rotating with pasture, hay, and grain crops which each relied on different qualities in the soil and allowed it time to recuperate. Now, specialist potato growers raised

Tobacco is cultivated in the sandy soils of the Montague region in eastern Kings.

crops two years out of three, with the result that the soil's humus broke down, eliminating its ability to retain moisture and making it vulnerable to erosion by wind and water.

This physical danger was matched by financial risk. The international potato market is notoriously fickle, and some specialists experienced heavy losses. Farmers learned the hard way that potato-growing was more of a gamble than mixed farming. This is why mixed farming has remained an important element in Island agriculture, as has now been recognized by the provincial government. Livestock and crop production complement each other, and farm receipts are more balanced.

One problem that has faced Island farmers is their remoteness from mar-

The Products

The Island has some 25 000 dairy cattle, fulfilling local needs in fluid and processed milk and contributing to a useful surplus of cheese and evaporated milk for export to the mainland.

In recent years hog production has been a valuable adjunct on many farms. Beef production, however, has not expanded as fast as it might, because prices have been unattractively low. There is a meat packing industry on the Island, and this produces for an export market which could be much increased.

As regards crops, grain is grown in all parts of the Island, particularly when linked with livestock operations. The Island is self-sufficient in grain production and should soon be in a position to export. Cash crops include a wide variety of vegetables, notably turnips and cole crops like cauliflower and broccoli. These are well suited to 'family farms,' where the whole

family is involved in cultivation and harvesting.

Many farmers cultivate certain crops in greenhouses before the start of spring, thus extending the 190-day outdoor growing season. One crop that responds well to this treatment is tobacco, which is grown in the sandy soils of the Montague area. Tobacco is a valuable export, but requires inten-

The dairy herd on the Island numbers some 25 000 animals, which makes the Island self-sufficient in dairy products and provides a small surplus for export.

sive cultivation, and therefore is relatively expensive to produce. Less demanding are the strawberry crop and the wild blueberry harvest.

Island farmers have been urged to concentrate on mixed farming of crops and livestock to offset wide fluctuations in the international potato market.

kets, particularly those of Central Canada, which in this century have been their mainstay. Ontario and Quebec have expanded domestic production and no longer depend on produce from the Maritimes. Besides, the cost of transport to such distant outlets has increased.

In response, Islanders have taken a new interest in the markets that were their chief support in the golden days of the shipbuilding era — the 'Boston states' of New England. Arrangements are in hand to take advantage of sea links with these areas, themselves adversely affected by high costs of transport from other parts of the United States.

In the summer season, many Island farms accommodate paying guests from the mainland. Visiting children like to help with the work.

25

The growing potato crop is regularly sprayed to stave off the twin threats of disease and insect pests.

Following ploughing, the farmer sows seed potatoes to produce a crop of table or process varieties or perhaps new seed potatoes for the export market.

SPUD ISLAND

Potatoes are to the Island what wheat is to Saskatchewan — a cornerstone of the economy. Rises and falls in the international market affect not only the farmers and processors directly involved in production, but ultimately the whole Island community.

Potatoes have been grown on the Island since the days of the French, when pioneers supplied produce for the garrison of Louisbourg. Crops thrived on land newly cleared of trees, planted among the stumps in holes made by mattocks or hoes. The temperate climate allowed plenty of time for the tubers to reach maturity.

With the British occupation, potato exports were switched to Newfoundland, Halifax, and the Miramichi in New Brunswick. From the 1830s, the arrival of many Irish settlers, to whom potato farming was a way of life, added to its importance. In periods of free trade, markets for Island potatoes and vegetables were developed in New England.

Until the beginning of the twentieth century, potato production was just one facet of mixed farming practised throughout the Island. But with the establishment of a provincial department of agriculture, a federal experimental farm, and a laboratory for researching plant disease, the great potential of the potato was realized.

Because the Island is an island, it was largely free of the pests and diseases which plagued production on the mainland. In 1916, when a few strains of Irish Cobblers and Green Mountains — then the chief varieties — were found to be virtually free of disease, a seed potato certification program was instituted. That gave rise to the great seed potato production industry, which has become the hallmark of Island agriculture. Varieties are grown not to be consumed, but to seed fields of table and process crops on other farms on the Island, or, more important, in Central Canada and in other countries.

Seed potato production is necessarily very specialized, and relatively small areas of land are involved, though these are appropriately more valuable. Only 30 per cent of the total potato hectarage is used for seed potato production, compared with 45 per cent for table (fresh) varieties and 25 per cent for process varieties.

Seed potato producers are supplied with certified seed from Fox Island, near Alberton, a former fox farm now operated by the P.E.I. Potato Marketing Board. Individual potato clones free of ring rot and viruses are the starting point of several years of planting and harvesting. Successive generations of potatoes are reclassified Elite I, Elite II, Elite III, Foundation, and Certified, as they progress. Island seed potatoes, with those of New Brunswick, make up nearly 90 per cent of Canada's total exports in this field — which are second only to those of the Netherlands.

This regional self-sufficiency, encouraged by the federal government, has had a far-reaching effect on the Island potato industry. Besides seed potatoes it has influenced the table crop, traditionally destined for Ontario. There, local competition has eroded Island farmers' share of the fresh market, and in addition they have been hard hit by the high cost of transport and by the growing popularity of processed foods.

Thus the Island farmers are coming to rely heavily on the processing industry, particularly concerns that freeze french fries and can new potatoes. French-fry production has expanded quickly in recent years, supplying the Canadian market and markets in many other countries. Waste from the french-fry process can be recycled as potato flakes and granules to make instant mashed potatoes.

In North America generally, half the potato crop is processed. On the Island the proportion is smaller but it is increasing. Besides adding value to the raw product, the processing greatly diminishes its weight and makes it more practical to transport at reasonable cost.

Critics of Island agriculture suggest that reliance on one root crop has been a mistake. They point out that the potato market is traditionally vulnerable to wide fluctuations, and suggest that crops like peas, turnips, parsnips, and, even more, cole crops would thrive as well as potatoes. Such crops yield much greater value per hectare.

If Island processors co-operate, it may be expected that Island agriculture will expand into many new fields.

Potatoes, particularly seed potatoes, are the Island's most valuable crop. Here a grader eliminates substandard potatoes from a newly-harvested consignment.

The potato harvest has profited from new technology that enables farmers to achieve more with less labour.

FORESTRY

Originally, the Island was covered by woodland so abundant that it drew high praise from Jacques Cartier. Visiting the Island in 1534, he and his men landed often to inspect the trees 'which were very beautiful and sweet-smelling, and we found them to be cedars, yews, pines, ashes, birches, elms, willows, and many others unknown to us.'

The trees were a hindrance to early settlers, but were a great boon to ship-builders of a later era. In selecting only the best trees, however, wood-cutters overlooked poor specimens and inferior species, which were the ancestors of the degenerate wood cover of today. Foresters say that most of what remains is of no possible use except as firewood.

Degenerate white spruce has come to account for one-half of the total wood cover on the Island, when once it amounted to no more than one tree in twenty. Foresters' one consolation is that the species is a favourite food of the spruce budworm, now present on the Island and promising to dispose of much of the unwanted tree cover.

Even so, foresters have made the white spruce the focus of their attention in a bold attempt to upgrade the quality of tree growth on the Island. They have scoured the woodlands for prime examples of the species — perhaps one tree in a million — and have collected seeds from those trees in an effort to develop a select strain.

The foresters seek trees that are perfectly straight and that have few branches to distract growth in the trunk but with existing limbs healthy. Such 'plus' trees often produce much less seed than do crooked, branchy examples, but their offspring are far superior, particularly if fertilized with pollen from trees of similar excellence.

Another means of improving Island tree growth is to graft scions from genetically sound trees on to root stock, raise them in a protected environment, and

One-half of the Island's wood cover is white spruce, and foresters say that most of it is of no use except as firewood. However, careful forest management is improving the quality of forest stands across the Island.

artificially fertilize them after two years. The idea is to treat the trees as large plants, and improve them as a farmer aims to improve his crops.

Not only white spruce is being improved. Island foresters have turned also to red spruce and yellow birch, again seeking prime genetic examples to initiate a seeding program. They prefer to opt for local trees rather than imported varieties, as Island conditions determine the success of their growth patterns.

Other rarer species will be reintroduced as time proceeds — for instance, the butternuts, which have almost completely disappeared, and the white and black ash and the red oak, which are now very rare. Genetic improvement will take many years, but the result will provide a valuable resource for future industrial activity where today there is none.

Improved forest products are not the only aim of the forestry program on the Island. The forest ecosystem has great influence on other aspects of the environment, and especially on agriculture. Tree cover provides an essential protection for soil and growing crops against winds blowing at more than 16 km/h.

Winds of such pace can have a three-way effect. They dry the soil, they knock plants against each other, and they dry the crop itself. At times the Island experiences winds of 45 or even 80 km/h, so the development of suitable windbreaks could be a great advantage. In addition, tree cover is a valuable safeguard against soil erosion.

A brisk sawmilling industry survived the great days of Island shipbuilding and still exists in spite of rapid depletion of viable timber resources. More than half of current production is from

A number of Island sawmills are still in operation, though not nearly as many as in the great days of the shipbuilding industry. Much of what the mills produce is used by the Island's construction industry.

a small handful of larger mills, but there are many smaller mills which operate only intermittently.

In making better use of the Island's forest resources, the government anticipates that many of the smaller mills will be phased out, though some will be expanded and modernized. The most promising forest area is located in Kings and eastern Queens, and on the Island as a whole, all but a few thousand hectares of forest land is in private hands.

29

FISHING

In 1534 Jacques Cartier complained that the Island had no harbours, but he confined his investigation to a short stretch of sandy coastline in the north-west corner. In reality the Island offers a number of bays and estuaries, which make perfect fishing havens.

The Island fishery first came into prominence in the eighteenth century, and the settlements of Saint Pierre and De Roma were related to it. The British took less interest, however, and concentrated on agriculture. It was left to American concerns to encourage the fishery during the reciprocal trade era of the 1850s and the 1860s.

In earlier days fishermen sought the codfish which filled the Gulf of St. Lawrence. However, it was found that the Island sun 'burned' cod drying on flakes, and that on the north coast,

blowing sand ruined the dressed fish. The Americans concentrated instead on mackerel, which they dried ashore and shipped to American markets.

Reciprocal trade with the United States ended in 1866, and the Americans were obliged to withdraw. But the processing establishments remained, among them not only drying and fish-oil plants, but also canning factories. It was these that first exploited the Island's most spectacular marine resource — the lobster population.

Originally there had been no means of preserving lobsters for market, and they were regarded as worthless—except by farmers, who gathered those driven ashore after a storm, ground them shells and all, and spread them on their land as fertilizer. But when markets opened in Britain and Europe, a major industry developed.

By 1900 lobsters accounted for half

Most Island fishermen are equipped with day-boats, which can be used for trapping lobsters, seining for herring, dragging for groundfish, or other purposes. Most boats are based in small harbours on the north, east, and south coasts.

the worth of the annual catch on the Island, and more than 200 small canneries were in operation. Nova Scotia and New Brunswick were able to ship live lobsters by rail to Central Canada and the United States. The first such shipment from the Island was despatched in 1927.

Today lobsters remain the mainstay of the Island fishing industry, though declining catches have long since made necessary the introduction of closed seasons and strict regulations regarding the catch. Currently some 1500 Island fishermen hold lobster fishing licences, though the Island government is lessening the number by purchasing the licences of those who voluntarily retire from the fishery.

Licences are issued in relation to the two Maritime lobster zones in which the Island falls. Each permits the operation of one boat and one fleet of traps — 300 in the northern zone and 250 in the

Pelagic fish like herring used to abound in the Gulf of St. Lawrence, but in recent years stocks have declined rapidly. Some are still caught by traditional purse-seining.

The bluefin tuna fishery is of growing importance. More than half the tuna fishing licences so far awarded in Eastern Canada have gone to the Island, either to commercial fishermen or to those who charter their boats to sports fishermen.

southern zone. The boat may be of any size, but on the Island most are day boats, nine to fourteen metres long, designed for inshore fishing.

In both zones the season lasts two months. The fisherman must check the length of each lobster's carapace, taken to be the section from the rear of the eye socket to the beginning of the tail section. The smallest are thrown back, the medium-sized are 'canners' destined for processing, and the largest are 'markets' to be sold live or cooked in the shell.

A proportion of the catch is cached in lobster pounds (large, saltwater tanks) in which the lobsters may be kept alive until required, then legally marketed out of season. Pounds are maintained to supply the lobster suppers which are a major tourist attraction.

Outside the lobster season, Island fishermen may opt for a range of alternative catches, but inevitably these are less valuable than the lobsters. Possible quarries include groundfish, like cod, redfish, hake, and flounder; pelagic fish, like mackerel and herring; or perhaps scallops dragged from the bottom.

A number of fishermen prefer the most exhilarating possibility — hunting the giant bluefin tuna. This fishery is as rigidly controlled as the lobster sector, and a licensed fisherman is restricted to two fish per boat per day. The Island is divided into two sections, each with a ten week open season.

Some tuna fishermen fish for the commercial market, but many have opted for the lucrative charter business in which they offer their boats and equipment to Islanders and tourists visiting the Island. By custom, all fish caught are retained by the licence holder and

most are processed for export to Japan, where red tuna meat is prized as a delicacy.

Most of the tuna boats are based at harbours along the Island's north shore. However, the ports of the east coast — Georgetown and Souris — depend on deep sea trawlers of modest size which operate in the Gulf of St. Lawrence, dragging and trawling for groundfish.

Souris has the only trawler fleet on the Island. Vessels spend several days on the fishing grounds, then return with their catch and offload at the processing plant. The Georgetown plant is serviced by vessels active throughout the Gulf and based in ports like Caraquet, New Brunswick, and North Sydney, Cape Breton.

Lobster fishing in the Maritimes is organized in districts, each with different rules affecting open seasons, minimum carapace length, and size of trap 'fleets' permissible for each licensed fisherman. This map outlines the requirements affecting carapace length.

A fisheries inspector measures a lobster's carapace — the section between eye socket and tail — to make sure it is not under size. If it is, it should be thrown back.

AQUACULTURE

There was a time when the Island's Malpeque oysters were even better known than its potatoes, at least among gourmets. Some authorities considered them the world's best. The oysters are still being fished, and still represent an important Island industry.

Strictly speaking, Malpeque is the picturesque bay in Prince which bites into the Island so deeply that its southern edge is barely seven kilometres from Bedeque Bay on the Island's south coast. Not all Malpeque oysters are from Malpeque, however. The name is applied to all Island oysters whether from Malpeque, Bedeque Bay, or the many other inlets where they thrive.

Oyster fishing is fascinating to watch. The fisherman sets out in a small dory and probes the mud on the bay's bottom with a giant pair of rake-ended tongs to catch up oysters found there. The tongs are five or six metres long, depending on the depth to be reached, and are worked like scissors.

The oyster fishery consists partly of leased areas, where the leaseholder has exclusive fishing rights, and partly of public areas, where any licence-holder may fish. Leaseholders quite literally 'farm' their holdings, spreading young seed oysters grown from 'spat' (baby oysters) and obtained by setting out spat collectors, and thinning and cultivating the beds to allow the oysters more

Sea Plants

The sea plant industry is of major importance on the west and north-eastern coasts. Irish moss can be dried and refined to produce the substance carrageenin, used as a stabilizer in food processing and other industries. The moss, light green to purple in colour and in appearance something like parsley, grows attached to rocks in depths of up to ten metres.

Each storm washes Irish moss ashore, and it is gathered by local families and transported to drying plants. From there it is eventually exported to refineries on the mainland. There are no restrictions on gathering this 'storm-tossed' weed, but restrictions do apply to harvesting Irish moss still growing on the rocks. The 'holdfast,' the thin disc by which the seaweed is attached, must not be damaged if the plant is to survive, and only the larger branches may be picked.

Sometimes Islanders harvest Irish moss by wading in from the beach.

Irish moss grows attached to rocks, and is harvested by gathering the larger branches with rakes, or by picking it up when the sea has washed it ashore. The moss is dried and refined to produce carrageenin, used as a stabilizer in food processing.

More often they approach it in small boats, hand-raking it into nets (in the north-east) or dragging rakes along the bottom (on the west and north-west coasts). For a time north-eastern fishermen dragged rakes too, but it was found that the rakes toppled rocks on to lobsters and killed them, and therefore the fishermen lost more money than they gained.

Canada's Atlantic provinces are the major world source of Irish moss, contributing up to 80 per cent of the total. More than half of Canada's production is from the Island. Many other sea plants are found in Island waters, each species with different properties, and it is possible that comparable industries will be developed around them.

Malpeque oysters — whether from Malpeque Bay or elsewhere on the Island — are renowned all over Canada and are considered by some to be the world's best.

Oyster farmers reach their crop by means of long-handled, rake-ended tongs which collect the oysters from mud on the bottom.

room, which improves their quality as they grow.

Oyster seed or brood stock for these operations may also be obtained from Malpeque Oyster Cultures Inc., a shellfish hatchery operated by the provincial government. Here oyster spat is cultivated to the point where it can be transferred to the oyster beds. Public beds are under the control of the federal government. However, a number of co-operative programs to improve the oyster fishery have been initiated by the province.

Oyster cultivation is one aspect of scientific 'aquaculture' which is expected to become a significant economic force on the Island. Aquaculture is underwater farming of shellfish, like scallops, mussels, oysters, and hard- and soft-shelled clams; fish, like Atlantic salmon and trout, which respond well to hatchery techniques; and even sea plants, like Irish moss.

Salmon and trout hatcheries are generally a federal responsibility, but shellfish production is provincial. Many of the shellfish occur naturally in Island waters, while other species are being introduced. Mussels, for instance, occur wild, but are of poor quality because of infestation by 'pearls' — clots formed around sand and other impurities. To overcome the problem and produce more meat, mussels are being cultivated on ropes suspended from rafts.

Scallops, too, are found naturally in Island waters, and are dragged from the bottom of Northumberland Strait. The Island has introduced a new species — the bay scallop from New England states. Soft-shell clams grow abundantly in Island waters, and clams from overcrowded sections are being transplanted to less populated areas with good growth potential. Hard-shell clams (quahaugs) are being reared at the province's shellfish hatchery for cultivation in suitable beds.

Soft-shell clams and mussels are harvested by Islanders and visitors, and their commercial potential is being exploited.

INDUSTRY

Islanders today bewail the high cost of manufactured goods imported from the mainland, but there was a time when the Island community was remarkably self-sufficient. Island directories of the 1860s provide long lists of local industries then in operation.

The directory for 1864, the year of the Charlottetown conference, records 123 boot and shoe makers, 104 blacksmiths, 47 carpenters and builders, 10 cabinet makers, 14 coopers, 55 tailors, 7 cloth mills, 42 grist mills, 45 sawmills, 7 brewers, 8 distillers, 12 wheelwrights, and various other local producers.

All this enterprise faded some time ago, the victim of competition from the machine era and mass-production on the mainland, which made patient craftsmanship redundant. Indeed, the Island was steadily transformed into one of Canada's 'have-not' provinces from the time it joined Confederation.

For many decades food processing, which lent itself to mechanization and for which the raw materials were close at hand, was the only significant manufacturing activity on the Island. But recent years have seen bold efforts to diversify, with heavy emphasis on the sensible notion that 'small is beautiful.'

The initiative came with the comprehensive development plan formulated by the Island government and DREE in 1969. Most of the plan's economic programs were concerned chiefly with agriculture, tourism, and fishing — the major revenue earners — but they opened the way for encouragement of local manufacturing.

The province's first priority has been to reduce costly importation to the Island by finding entrepreneurs prepared to manufacture equivalent articles on the spot. From this follows a search for outside markets to allow these local entrepreneurs to expand production. The greatest potential lies in high-value, low-weight commodities that are not handicapped by the high cost of transport.

The third step — and the most difficult — is to attract specialist manufacturers catering not to local markets, but for national and international distribution. Here the Island is in competition with provinces and municipalities across Canada, but so far it has had considerable success. By devising programs to suit businesses which elsewhere might be considered too small to deserve help, the Island has given them their start. Examples include a pottery and firms making sunglasses and computerized calibrators.

The chief thrust of the industrial program is directed through the prestigious industrial parks established at West Royalty outside Charlottetown and at Summerside. Each park is equipped with an industrial mall in which small businesses may rent space, giving them a chance to prove themselves without having to risk large sums of capital in land or buildings. If they fail, little is lost; if they succeed, they expand at their own pace and eventually move to their own premises.

Another quite unrelated inducement to manufacturers to locate on the Island has been the level of labour stability. The Island loses fewer working days through industrial disputes than any other area in Canada, chiefly because negotiation between management and employees is more relaxed than in situations where much larger numbers of workers are involved.

Outside the industrial parks, most manufacturing is concerned with food processing. Most fish processing plants operate on a seasonal basis, but plants handling agricultural products, notably potatoes, work year-round. The Island is also noted for milling wool, a tradition from the days when there was a significant sheep population. Now much of the raw material comes from Nova Scotia and Cape Breton.

In addition, there have been steps taken to revive cottage industry in rural areas. Some enterprises, notably home quilting and weaving, are already established, and several craft co-operatives are in production. Furniture making and pottery have been influenced by mainland craftsmen who have settled on the Island.

Two home industries which never really died out are lobster-trap manufacture and basket making. At one time plastic traps were introduced, but fishermen found that they did not work properly and preferred to rely on their own efforts. Baskets of split ash are made by Micmac Indians, particularly by the bands on Lennox Island.

The rising value of fish justifies the continued existence of the Island's boat-building industry, which produces multipurpose day-boats able to catch many varieties.

Island fish processing plants are seasonal. Some handle only one product, such as lobster; some process a variety of species. Here Island lobsters are boiled prior to canning.

Potato processing has emerged as a major Island industry, following a swing in tastes across North America. Processed frozen foods are favoured more than fresh products which require home preparation. Here potatoes emerge from a peeler at a plant in New Annan, between Summerside and Kensington, before being sliced as french fries.

Scheduled services of Air Canada and Eastern Provincial Airways connect the Island with the other Maritime provinces and with the rest of Canada. Charlottetown airport is especially busy during the holiday season.

CN Marine operates ferries between Borden and Cape Tormentine in New Brunswick. The service runs year-round, and fulfils one of the conditions under which the Island joined Confederation.

The Island's narrow-gauge railway, built during the 1870s, runs from one end of the Island to the other. It is operated by Canadian National and carries only freight.

TRANSPORTATION

The Island is nearly 15 km from Cape Tormentine in New Brunswick, the nearest point on the mainland. For almost five months each winter Northumberland Strait is blocked by moving ice, which has been an immense handicap since the time of early settlement.

Before 1827, the Island's single link with the mainland during winter was a twice-monthly courier service over the ice between Wood Islands on the south-east shore and Pictou in Nova Scotia. Later, small ice boats with runners were introduced to make the crossing from Cape Traverse (near Borden) to Cape Tormentine. The boats could be sailed or rowed where ice conditions allowed, but needed considerable man-handling while being slid over the ice on runners. Different fares were charged — one for passengers ready to help with the man-handling, getting out on the ice and heaving on a body-strap, and a higher one for inactive passengers. Boats usually travelled in convoy.

During the 1860s private steamers ran scheduled services to mainland ports during summer, but only the ice boats could make the trip during winter. Lengthy winter isolation was a major factor in persuading the Island legislature to turn down suggestions of Maritime union, because the Island had little to gain from public works projects carried out on the mainland partly at the Island's expense.

Similar objections were raised when federal union was discussed in 1864. In 1869 the new Dominion government offered 'better terms,' including 'efficient steam service' to operate both winter and summer, and so link the Island with mainland railways. These terms were rejected by the Island because the Dominion would not agree to the Island's demands over land settlement.

In the event, it was another transportation issue that brought the Island into Confederation — the need for help with financing construction of the new Island railway. But the Island insisted on year-round steamer service as a condition to its entering the Dominion, and the *Northern Light*, a wooden ice-breaker, was introduced in 1876.

The *Northern Light* and its successors provided indifferent service for some decades. It seemed that the Dominion government took its responsibilities less than seriously. Not until 1917 was an efficient car ferry (for rail cars) introduced, though such a service had been suggested as early as the 1880s.

Today, however, the ferry service is relatively efficient. CN Marine is expected to provide year-round, regular service both day and night between Borden and Cape Tormentine, carrying both rail and road transport. In summer and fall a private company is contracted to operate ferries between Wood Islands and Caribou, near Pictou, Nova Scotia, but this service is suspended during winter.

Strangely, the Island serves as 'mainland' for a community even more isolated — the islanders of the Magdalens in the middle of the Gulf of St. Lawrence, administered as part of Quebec. A ferry serving the Magdalens departs from Souris, which is one reason why Quebec licence plates are a common sight on Island roads.

The improved ferry service between the Island and the mainland has been matched by rapid improvements in the highway system. There is a paved road network more extensive than any other province's, considering the Island's size, and in general roads are in good repair. A section of the Trans-Canada Highway runs from Borden to Wood Islands by way of Charlottetown.

The chief port on the Island is Charlottetown, which has a fine natural harbour off Hillsborough Bay. Other ports include Summerside, Souris, and Georgetown.

Now, road traffic almost totally overshadows the Island railway. This is ironic, because from the time gasoline-powered vehicles were introduced to the Island in 1905, they were considered a menace to life and property. In 1908 the Island legislature banned them. Public opinion relented only slowly, and the automobile was not fully accepted on the Island until it proved its worth during World War I.

At various times the Island's vulnerability has been demonstrated by breaks in the ferry service — notably by a strike in 1973. At such times Islanders have agitated for a more reliable link with the mainland, for instance, a tunnel or causeway. In 1962 the federal Conservative government, led by John Diefenbaker, announced that a causeway would be constructed. However, successive Liberal governments hesitated to put the plan into effect when they realized what it would cost.

Meanwhile, public opinion on the Island began to change. Massive annual influxes of visitors were arriving from the mainland by ferry. Many Islanders believed that a causeway would bring even more, and that they might soon find themselves outnumbered. In 1976 the provincial government quietly announced that the Island preferred to remain what it was.

TOURISM

All Canada's provinces have come to lay heavy emphasis on tourism as a key element in their economies, but none more than the Island. There, tourism has long ranked second in importance after agriculture, though it is now being overtaken by manufacturing.

The Island's tourist industry has its roots far back in the nineteenth century, when a number of seaside resorts were in operation, most notably Rustico on the north shore. Relatively small numbers of visitors came, but they were joined by Islanders who had settled on the mainland, returning home to visit families and friends. As decades passed, the annual tide of these exiles became considerable.

Even today, non-resident Islanders make an important contribution to the tourist industry, particularly during Charlottetown's 'Old Home Week' and Summerside's 'Lobster Carnival,' which are largely designed for their benefit. But now they are greatly outnumbered by visitors who have no connection with the Island.

As in other provinces, the tourist industry began to flourish during the 'leisure revolution' of the 1950s and the 1960s, when families found that they had enough time and money to travel. The Island quickly became a favourite goal for mainland Canadians, particularly those from Nova Scotia and New Brunswick.

Its attractions were many. Its beaches and sea bathing were the finest in Canada. Its red soil and rolling green farmland in spring and summer and the glorious fall colour seemed more beautiful than anything found on the mainland. Not least, it was an island, normally attainable only through the romance of a sea crossing.

Soon a pattern was established. Visitors congregated in the Island's central core, a triangle in Queens with Charlottetown as its apex and the Prince Edward Island National Park along the north coast as its base. It was in this area that hotels, camp sites, and tourist attractions were developed.

More than anything, visitors appreciated the beaches. Most favoured those of the north shore, especially the stretch in the national park, charac-

Some vacationing families dig clams from the beach, build a fire, and bake them on the spot.

The Woodleigh Replicas at Burlington are large-scale models of famous cathedrals, castles, and other buildings of historic importance. This is York Minster.

terized by white sand. Islanders, on the other hand, preferred those along the south shore, where the sand is red but the water is appreciably warmer.

The national park is one of Canada's smallest, stretching some 40 km along the shore but only a short distance inland, and in area not much more than 18 km². However, it has proved the second most popular in Canada, after Banff in Alberta. Not least of its attractions is the Anne of Green Gables homestead and the golf course at Cavendish.

There are indications, however, that the central triangle that is so popular with tourists has reached its saturation point, and the provincial government has been working to spread the benefits of the industry farther afield. The first step has been construction of a new resort at Brudenell on the east coast, which is equipped to serve as a convention centre. A similar resort is coming into being at Mill River on the west coast. Both are government-run, though ordinarily the province prefers to leave the creation of facilities to private enterprise.

Another means of inducing visitors to try new areas of the Island is by promoting three scenic drives, each designed as a day trip and avoiding the principal highways but taking in the prime attractions. The shortest, the Blue Heron Drive in the central core, leads from the north shore beaches to the south shore seascapes.

In the west, the Lady Slipper Drive flows through Prince like a figure eight, visiting both Acadian communities in the south and the Indian community of Lennox Island on the north coast near Alberton. In the east, the Kings Byway takes in fishing communities including North Lake, billed as the world's tuna fishing capital.

One major difficulty that the Island faces is that its tourist season is very short — a matter of two months each year at the height of summer, the period of school holidays. This is a pity, because one of the Island's most attractive seasons is fall, lasting well into October. Early summer is also pleasant, with the landscape green and fresh.

The white sands of Prince Edward Island National Park are a major draw for mainland vacationers. Most Islanders, however, prefer less crowded conditions on the many other beaches along the coasts.

One-price lobster suppers, pioneered by Island service clubs and social organizations, provide visitors with an opportunity to sample fine home cooking.

ENERGY

Until 1977 the Island relied on oil imports for 98 per cent of its energy needs, including electrical power generation. But the fast-rising cost of oil forced the Island government to develop new energy sources and to pioneer energy conservation.

The high cost of electricity on the Island has been a bone of contention for some time, and it was in this area that the first moves were made. The federal government and the province agreed to lay a submarine power cable linking the Island with New Brunswick.

In summer 1977 two 21-km cables were laid, stretching from Richmond Cove on the Island to Murray Corner in New Brunswick. Two cables were laid in case the first malfunctioned. Each was buried in a trench on the seabed to protect it from damage by drift ice or fishing operations.

The cables belong to the province, but the power they convey is the property of Maritime Electric, the Island utility, which buys it from the New

Brunswick Electric Power Commission under a thirty-year contract.

At the present rate of consumption, the cable link provides 80 or 90 per cent of the Island's minimum night load — in other words, its lightest requirement. Maritime Electric's own oil-and-gas-fired generators provide additional power as needed. Power is distributed throughout the Island by an integrated grid.

Besides importing mainland power, the Island has introduced a program of house insulation to cut down on power used for space heating — a large part of the load. It has also sought new, cheap energy sources at home, not so much to lower energy costs as to prevent them from rising. In this search the Island is handicapped by its geography and its population — the former too flat to offer possibilities of significant hydroelectrical generation, the latter too small to justify a nuclear installation. Instead the province rests its hopes on its Institute of Man and Resources, an independent agency funded by the province and other sources.

The institute was created to explore

and test strategies to counter the Island's dependence on non-renewable resources, imported manufactured goods, and external subsidies. But its formation coincided with the energy crisis, and its first major challenge was the energy problem. It quickly identified three potential energy sources present on the Island in quantity — wind and sun, being explored in many parts of the world, and a source not often regarded as important: waste woodlands, the product of degenerate white spruce which had invaded all parts of the Island.

The institute's work was complemented by a quite separate scheme at Spry Point in eastern Kings, the Ark, a self-sufficient life-support unit built with a federal grant. The Ark is a project of the New Alchemy Institute of Massachusetts, which is devoted to testing non-exploitative modes of living. Officially opened in 1976, the Ark relies almost completely on solar and wind power and is capable of meeting all the food and energy needs of a small family. It consists of a greenhouse, a dwelling unit, and two dozen fish-growing tanks. A family is in residence, and scientists make regular visits.

Electrical power for the Ark is provided by windmills, and any surplus is fed into the Island power grid. Solar panels on the roof heat all units and particularly the fish ponds. During winter, supplementary heat may be produced by a stove burning wood from the surrounding forest.

The Ark is directly relevant to future North American lifestyle, but most of all to the Island community, which has a tradition of self-supporting family units. Perhaps the general introduction of units like the Ark is still far in the future, but it will be no surprise if Islanders are among the first to adopt them.

In summer 1977 the cable-laying barge Mulus IV laid a submarine power cable to link the Island with New Brunswick. The cable was stored on large carousels and paid out as the barge progressed. Tugs and its own anchors held the barge in position above a trench previously dug on the seabed.

The Ark at Spry Point in eastern Kings is a self-sufficient life-support unit, relying almost completely on solar and wind energy. It was officially opened in 1976.

Thermal generating plants at Charlottetown and Borden supplement the electric power imported from New Brunswick by submarine cable. This is the oil-fired station in Charlottetown.

The power cable laid across Northumberland Strait was made in Sweden, and is 128 mm in diameter. The three conductors are insulated and protected within a sheath of lead alloy, and the cable is armoured by steel wire and oil-impregnated jute.

Murray River, in south-eastern Kings, was formerly a shipbuilding village, but is now the distribution centre for the surrounding farming community.

Islanders in rural districts regard Charlottetown as 'the big city,' though by mainland standards its size is modest. Prominent in the city centre are St. Dunstan's Cathedral and, almost hidden behind it, Province House. To the left is the Confederation Centre of the Arts.

COMMUNITIES

According to the 1976 Statistics Canada mini-census, the Island's population was 118 229, making it Canada's most densely populated province. Even so, it is far from crowded, and retains all its old rural charm.

In general terms one-third of the population lives on farms throughout the Island. Another third lives in hamlets and villages — small service centres like Crapaud, Hunter River, and Mount Stewart that cater to the local neighbourhood, and fishing villages along the coast like Murray Harbour, North Rustico, and St. Peters.

Only one-third of the population lives in centres larger than 1000 people. The biggest is Charlottetown, the Island's capital and commercial hub. Including its suburbs, Parkdale and Sherwood, Greater Charlottetown holds more than 25 000 people. Summerside holds about 10 000, and no other town tops 2000.

The Charlottetown area has been the focal point of Island life since the time of French occupation. Named after Queen Charlotte, George III's consort, Charlottetown proper was founded in 1763 on the site chosen for the Island capital by Capt. Samuel Holland. It was incorporated in 1855.

Today Charlottetown prospers as the Island's seat of government and educational centre, quite apart from its commercial significance as chief port and banking centre. Its pace is never unduly fast, but at all times of the year things are happening — particularly in summer, when the tourists arrive and the city's cultural life is in full swing.

This cultural activity revolves around the Confederation Centre of the Arts, which houses a modern theatre, art gallery, and library, and also the Island's public archives. It is most unusual for a city of Charlottetown's size to have such sophisticated facilities, and they are not wasted. A three-month festival is held each summer, and many other events are organized in the course of the year.

The Confederation Centre is located in the heart of the city, next to Province House, which is the Island's most significant historic site. Between it and the waterfront is 'Old Charlottetown,' cur-

Georgetown, named for King George III, is the county town of Kings. It is best known as a shipbuilding and fish processing centre.

rently undergoing a facelift in a bid to revitalize the city's heart.

Another interesting building is Government House, the official home of Island lieutenant-governors since the 1830s, sited west of the city centre in Victoria Park. Close by is the headquarters of the provincial administration, Charlottetown's biggest employer. Here and elsewhere in the city, streets are lined by trees and are most attractive.

Summerside's history as a community is much shorter than Charlottetown's, though its first settler, Daniel Green, a Loyalist, made his home there in 1785. Its site was called 'Green's Shore' — less flatteringly, 'the swamp' — and it was a landing place for travellers proceeding between Bedeque and St. Eleanors inland, then Prince's county seat.

In 1851 the shipbuilder J. C. Pope moved his concern from Bedeque to Green's Shore, and the elements of a village took shape around it. Developing water communication with the mainland and the extension of the railways to the New Brunswick coast at Shediac strengthened Summerside's claim to be Prince's economic capital.

The town was incorporated in 1877, and today prospers as the Island's second largest community. Much of its population is of French descent. Summerside relies on its position as distribution centre, port, and seat of government, and in recent years its waterfront area has been extensively redeveloped. Among the new buildings are the Prince Edward Island Marine and Fisheries Training Centre and a cultural centre.

The third county seat on the Island is Georgetown in Kings. It is small compared with the others, but is developing as a shipbuilding centre, thanks to government investment. Not far away is the Island's third biggest town, Montague, which is important as the centre of the prosperous tobacco belt.

Souris, also in Kings, is significant as a fishing centre and as the terminal of the Island's ferry link with the Magdalen islands. In Prince, Kensington and St. Eleanors are both distribution centres, the latter serving a major Canadian Forces Base nearby.

Alberton and Tignish, in the far north of Prince, are remote from the rest of the Island and have developed their own traditions. Tignish, a settlement where Acadians and Islanders of Irish descent live in harmony, is noted particularly for co-operative movements involving the whole community.

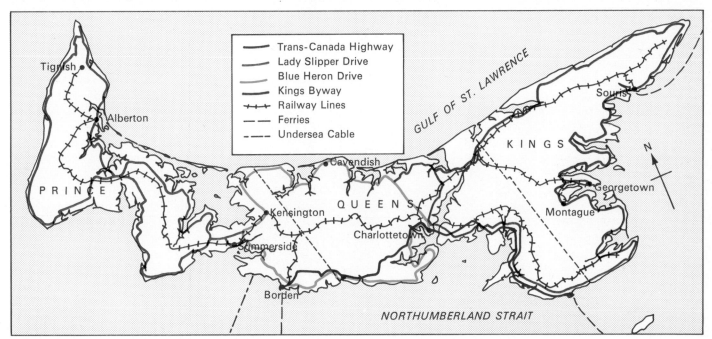

GOVERNMENT

Provincial governments in Canada consist of three divisions, as does the federal government: a legislature which makes laws, an executive which puts them into effect, and a judiciary which interprets them. The Island's government is no exception. Of course, it is much smaller in scale than the norm, but all the institutions found in other provinces are present on the Island too. Island government is a microcosm of the systems used elsewhere, and provides valuable insights into their strengths and weaknesses.

As in the other provinces, the government is headed by the Queen's representative, the lieutenant-governor. He or she is normally appointed in recognition of past services to the province. The lieutenant-governor has a variety of functions, the most important of them being the signing of bills passed by the Assembly to make them law.

The lieutenant-governor and the Assembly together form the legislature. Following an election, the lieutenant-governor invites the leader of the winning party to form a government, that is, an executive council, or cabinet, which both advises the lieutenant-governor and joins him in promulgating ordinances and making appointments.

The executive council is composed of members of the Assembly who are appointed ministers of the Crown, pledged to serve the Queen. Normally each is given charge of one or more government departments which carry

out the instructions of the executive. Each department is headed by a professional civil servant, a deputy minister.

On the Island, the executive council usually has no more than nine or ten members. Half are responsible to the legislature for at least two departments. Depending on the government in power, there are normally about a dozen departments, most of them concerned with economic and industrial matters or social concerns.

The economic and industrial departments are Finance, Industry and Commerce, Agriculture and Forestry, Fisheries, Labour, and Development. Departments handling social concerns are Education, Health, and Social Services. In addition there are Municipal Affairs, Justice, Public Works, Highways, Environment, Tourism, Parks and Conservation, and the Department of the Provincial Secretary.

Besides 'line' departments, the executive council may establish Crown commissions and agencies to investigate or administer particular spheres requiring specialist treatment. Examples on the Island are the Hospital and Health Services Commission and the Land Use Commission.

All these departments and agencies compete for the funds voted annually by the legislature (and derived from provincial taxation and other revenues and from federal cost-sharing programs). Priorities are assessed by the provincial Treasury Board, part of the Department of Finance, which acts as a committee of the executive.

The Island's executive council in session. At the head of the table is the Island's premier, Hon. Alexander Campbell.

There is a third element of provincial government, remote from the others. This is the judiciary, the bench of judges appointed by the federal government (to the Island Supreme Court) or by the lieutenant-governor-in-council (to provincial courts). The court system was radically reformed in 1975 and 1976. As a result, an old intermediate level of 'county courts' was merged with the Supreme Court based in Charlottetown. Judges of the Supreme Court visit Summerside and Georgetown 'on assize,' so that these centres retain their old significance as county seats. Besides, the reforms produced Canada's first comprehensive family court.

As elsewhere, the provincial government is the middle of three tiers, each with carefully delineated responsibilities. Most departments of the federal government are represented on the Island, and the headquarters of the dwindling Department of Veterans Affairs is being moved from Ottawa to Charlottetown.

The bottom tier, municipal government, is carried out by the elected mayor and aldermen of Charlottetown, the mayors and councillors of the various other towns, and the commissioners of incorporated villages. They have charge of such municipal services as water, sewage and garbage disposal, snow clearance, and sometimes police.

The Premiers

Island elections have been fought by the Liberals (L), political heirs of the old reformers, and the Conservatives (C), heirs of the landowners and since 1942 known as the Progressive Conservatives (PC). The Liberals have had much the best of these encounters, though the popular vote has been evenly split between the two parties.

Here is a list of Island premiers since Confederation in 1873.

J. C. Pope (C)	1873
L. C. Owen (C)	1873 – 1876
L. H. Davies (L)	1876 – 1879
W. W. Sullivan (C)	1879 – 1889
N. McLeod (C)	1889 – 1891
F. Peters (L)	1891 – 1897
A. B. Warburton (L)	1897 – 1898
D. Farquharson (L)	1898 – 1901
A. Peters (L)	1901 – 1908
F. L. Haszard (L)	1908 – 1911
James Palmer (L)	1911
John A. Mathieson (C)	1911 – 1917
Aubin A. Arsenault (C)	1917 – 1919
J. H. Bell (L)	1919 – 1923
James D. Stewart (C)	1923 – 1927
Albert C. Saunders (L)	1927 – 1930
Walter M. Lea (L)	1935 – 1936
Thane A. Campbell (L)	1936 – 1943
J. Walter Jones (L)	1943 – 1953
Alexander W. Matheson (L)	1953 – 1959
Walter R. Shaw (PC)	1959 – 1966
Alexander B. Campbell (L)	1966 –

The Island's public service contains all the elements found in other provinces but in miniature. Most departments are accommodated in the Provincial Building, Charlottetown.

The Island Judiciary was reformed in 1975 and 1976 and consists of the Supreme Court and the provincial court.

Shaw   **Campbell**

Government House in Charlottetown's Victoria Park, the official home of the lieutenant-governor, was built in the 1830s.

Province House, formerly the Colonial Building, is still the seat of the Island legislature. The building was first used in 1848 and originally housed both Assembly and Council sitting separately, until 1893 when the two bodies were merged.

THE ASSEMBLY

The Island's thirty-two-member Legislative Assembly is like no other in Canada. It is the result of the amalgamation of the two chambers that comprised the legislature until 1893, and to this day it retains a distinction between 'assemblymen' and 'councillors.'

In practice there is no longer any difference in status between the two, except that they are elected separately in each of the Island's ridings. But the distinction is a reminder of a most unorthodox political history, which continues to surface at election time. By custom, many ridings deliberately return one Protestant and one Catholic.

The Island's Assembly first sat in 1773 in a Charlottetown tavern, a motley gathering that, according to tradition, prompted the tavern doorkeeper to remark: 'This is a damned queer parliament!' He was summarily expelled for disrespect. The Assembly had been elected, but the Legislative Council with which it worked was nominated by the governor.

The Island was granted responsible government in 1851, and soon afterwards the Council was reformed to become an elected body. By that time the Assembly consisted of thirty members, two from each of five constituencies in each county. Constituencies were numbered rather than named — for instance, 1st, 2nd, 3rd, and 4th Kings (all rural) and 5th Kings (Georgetown, the county town).

Since 1847 the legislature had sat in the Colonial Building in Charlottetown, today's Province House. The Assembly's chamber was at one end, the Council's at the other. Like other provinces, the Island decided to improve legislative efficiency by resorting to only one chamber. In 1893 a compromise was reached by which the two chambers united, though elsewhere Councils were abolished. The number of assemblymen was pruned to fifteen to balance the number of councillors.

From that time, each constituency elected one assemblyman and one councillor, in many cases resorting to a religious compromise. Elections were a two-way contest between Liberals and Conservatives, and where a Liberal Protestant faced a Conservative Protestant

for the assemblyman's seat, two Catholics fought to be councillor.

There was no constitutional provision for this arrangement, but it is still observed in nine of the sixteen current ridings. Precise traditions vary. In one constituency the assemblyman may be Protestant and the councillor Catholic, but in a neighbouring riding it may be the other way around.

Until 1963 the situation was further complicated by the qualifications required of voters. The right to vote for the assemblyman was held by residents of the constituency (subject to an age qualification and until 1922 a sex qualification as well) or by those owning property situated in the constituency and worth more than $100.

This amounted to universal suffrage (at least after 1922, when women were given the vote). As regards councillors, however, the right to vote was restricted to those owning property in the riding worth more than $350. Technically, if a couple owned property worth that much in each of the fifteen constituencies, they were entitled to sixty votes between them.

The province's Legislative Assembly consists of thirty-two councillors and assemblymen representing sixteen ridings. In the Assembly chamber, the government sits to the Speaker's left, rather than to his right as in all other provincial legislatures apart from Newfoundland's.

All that was changed in 1963, following a redistribution of seats which divided the old 5th Queens (Charlottetown) into two new ridings, increasing the size of the Assembly to thirty-two seats. The old property qualifications were swept away and suffrage now depends on residence, citizenship, and age.

The Assembly sits every spring, and if necessary for a few days in fall as well. Visitors familiar with the usual parliamentary custom by which the government sits to the Speaker's right note that on the Island (as in Newfoundland) it sits to his left. Some say that an early government discovered that the left hand side of the chamber was warmer.

HEALTH AND EDUCATION

As in other provinces, a high proportion of the Island government's funds is spent on social services including health, hospitals, and education. Each service has a long history, but in recent years has been subject to wholesale reorganization to meet modern needs.

The education system in particular has always been prominent. Until the 1950s Island communities were all served by small district schools, in most cases staffed by a single teacher, accommodated in one or two rooms, and overseen by three local trustees. They have been immortalized in Lucy Maud Montgomery's *Anne* books.

In those schools students of all ages studied together, but were given individual attention by the teacher. The goal of many was to be admitted to Prince of Wales College or the Roman Catholic St. Dunstan's College in Charlottetown, or in later years to the high school established in Summerside.

From the mid-1950s, however, the Island government encouraged the formation of regional high schools across the province, until in the later 1960s there were seventeen of them. In the 1960s and early 1970s, the province began to consolidate the little community schools, in the interests of more efficient tuition.

Not all Islanders were glad to see the passing of the old district schools, and

their buildings are still to be seen throughout the Island. They had been a focus of community life, and many believed that student busing to the new consolidated schools somehow destroyed local loyalties. On the other hand, the personal character of Island education has not been lost, in that the Island still has the lowest student-teacher ratio in Canada.

As part of the consolidation, the old system of 217 independent community school boards was abandoned in 1972, in favour of five regional school boards covering geographic units. The smallest, Unit 5 in the south-west, is French-medium and offers tuition in that language with gradual introduction to English. Each of the English-medium school boards has organized French immersion courses in certain schools.

Educational reform was carried through at post-secondary level, too. Following the report of a government commission in 1969, Prince of Wales College and St. Dunstan's were merged to become the University of Prince Edward Island. At the same time the government established Holland College, which offers courses in applied arts and technology.

Hospital services used to be as much a part of community life as the school system, but it must be admitted that hospitals were established on a 'hit or miss' basis by communities which felt that they were needed. Fortunately they

were evenly spaced, though Charlottetown came to possess two — one Protestant, one Roman Catholic.

Resources of the two Charlottetown hospitals are being merged into a single referral hospital to serve the whole Island. There is another referral hospital in Summerside, and small community hospitals in Alberton, O'Leary, and Tyne Valley in the west, and Montague and Souris in the east. Each of these hospitals is administered by a board elected from members of the corporation that owns it, though since 1959 all have been funded by the province through its hospitals commission, out of the general revenue. This means that Islanders pay no hospital insurance, and their medicare is also free.

A community as small as the Island's cannot support advanced specialist facilities, and complicated cases are referred to the mainland — most often to Halifax, since the majority of Island doctors are graduates of Dalhousie University medical school. But some difficult cases are referred to specialists in Montreal or Boston.

General hospital services and the medicare program are administered separately from the Island Department of Health, which is chiefly involved in deterrent programs designed to stamp out infectious diseases and other avoidable maladies. These preventive programs include vaccination schemes, dental treatment, cancer diagnosis, and mental health care. The department also runs an isolation hospital and homes for special care.

The Department of Health's work is closely correlated with that of the Departments of Social Services and of the Environment. The Department of Social Services was set up in 1972 to cope with new pressures in child and family relations, rehabilitation, services for the aged, and income security. The Department of the Environment acts as government watchdog in staving off pollution.

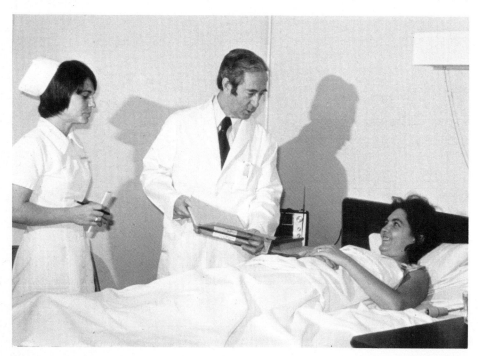

Islanders do not pay hospital insurance, since hospital services are funded out of the provincial government's general revenue. Medicare — physicians' services and certain prescribed drugs and equipment — is also free.

Young students meet a guidance teacher at an Island elementary school. The Island has the lowest student-teacher ratio of any province in Canada.

Holland College of Applied Arts and Technology, the Island's community college, which incorporates the Atlantic Police College, training police from communities in the Atlantic provinces.

A French class in progress at a junior high school in Charlottetown. Each of the Island's four English-medium school boards offers French immersion courses in certain schools.

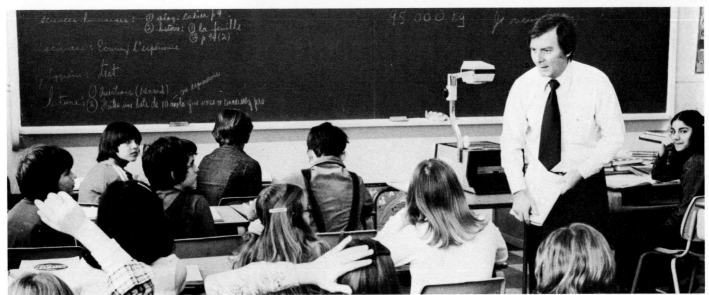

Confederation Centre Art Gallery

One of several self-portraits by Robert Harris, who was born in Wales in 1849 but was an Island resident from 1856. A large number of Harris's works are held by the Confederation Centre Art Gallery.

The most noted literary figure produced by the Island has been Lucy Maud Montgomery, author of the Anne books among many others.

Confederation Centre of the Arts Photo

The Confederation Centre of the Arts Boys' Choir has toured Canada and the United States. Founded in 1973, the choir recruits members from many communities.

ISLAND CULTURE

To date Canada has produced only one classic children's tale to rank with the likes of *Alice's Adventures in Wonderland* and *The Adventures of Tom Sawyer*. It is Lucy Maud Montgomery's *Anne of Green Gables*, and it was written on the Island.

Lucy Maud — as many Islanders refer to her — was born at Clinton in northern Queens in 1874. Her mother died soon after her birth, and when her father moved to Saskatchewan to take up a business position, she was taken in by her grandparents. They lived in Cavendish, and there she attended the local school. Later she qualified as a teacher and taught in several schools elsewhere on the Island.

Many of the adventures Lucy Maud had in these years were later incorporated in her *Anne* books. The first, *Anne of Green Gables*, was published in 1908, and she had written two sequels by 1911 when she married Rev. Ewan MacDonald, a fellow Islander. The couple soon moved to Ontario and there Lucy Maud wrote many more books.

However, it was her first effort that assured her success, and it is still read all over the world. Lucy Maud's work excited awareness of the Island throughout Canada and, indeed, far beyond. More recently, so has the work of the Island poet Milton Acorn, at least in Canada.

Originally a carpenter, Acorn was persuaded to write full-time, and admirers had dubbed him Canada's 'People's Poet.' Ironically, he too moved to Ontario following early success, but his poetry creates a warm picture of the Island's special character. It is symptomatic of fierce pride in all that the Island stands for.

For most of its history the Island had to rely on its own resources to sustain its cultural existence, but a private initiative connected with the centenary of the Charlottetown conference of 1864 produced a dramatic change. Provinces across Canada were induced to contribute to a suitable memorial to 'the cradle of Confederation.'

The result was the Charlottetown Confederation Centre of the Arts, a cultural complex in which all Canadians have a stake. Actual celebration of the conference's centenary revolved around a summer festival staged in the centre. It was decided to make the festival an annual event, and in 1965 it staged a musical version of *Anne of Green Gables*, which proved an immediate hit.

Since its debut, *Anne* has been revived each year at the festival, and has four times toured Canada. It has been staged in London, on Broadway, and in Japan. *Anne's* success prompted the festival to specialize in Canadian musicals. Each year three are presented, at least one of them a new work.

Out of season, the centre is used for concerts and performances by Islanders, among them a noted boys' choir based at the centre which has several times toured regions of Canada and the United States. The Atlantic Symphony Orchestra pays occasional visits, and professional theatre companies and entertainers visiting the Maritimes often include Charlottetown on their itineraries.

The Charlottetown Centre art gallery is regarded as one of Canada's most prominent. Its permanent collection includes fine arts and crafts representing all regions of Canada, but is most famous for a rich selection of works by Robert Harris, the most accomplished painter the Island has produced.

Harris was born in Wales, but arrived on the Island in 1856 at the age of seven. His father ran a lobster and pork packing plant at Murray Harbour. On leaving school, Harris was employed as a land surveyor and visited many remote parts of the Island. In his spare time he taught himself to paint. In 1873 Harris decided to make painting his career, and studied in Boston, London, and Paris.

Returning to Canada, Harris established a studio in Toronto, and became known as Canada's leading portrait artist. His most notable commission was to paint a record of the 1864 Quebec conference — the painting famous as *The Fathers of Confederation*. He

A musical version of *Anne of Green Gables* was first staged at the Charlottetown Festival of 1965 and proved an immediate hit, and is revived at the festival every year. Here Elizabeth Mawson appears as Marilla (right), Malorie-Ann Spiller as Anne, and George Merner as Matthew. The Charlottetown Summer Festival is produced by the Fathers of Confederation Buildings Trust.

periodically returned to the Island, and when he died in 1917 he was buried in Charlottetown.

No other Island painter has achieved Harris's stature, but the local attractions have long acted as a magnet to painters, writers, and other creative artists from outside. They and not a few Islanders have worked quietly at what interests them, and have made the most of an ideal environment.

The Confederation Centre of the Arts in Charlottetown was opened in 1964 to celebrate the centenary of the Charlottetown conference. The centre includes a theatre, art gallery, and library, and was the first such complex built in Canada.

Confederation Centre of the Arts Photo

61289

SPORT

Amateur sport on the Island — there is no professional sport, apart from harness racing — is administered by an autonomous body known as Sport P.E.I. Its membership includes nearly forty sports-governing bodies.

These bodies control a broad spectrum of Island sports, everything from badminton and soccer to sailing and synchronized swimming. But what is remarkable is that their combined membership adds up to nearly 30 000, about a quarter of the total of the Island's population. That is a far higher proportion than in any other province.

Of course, the figure is misleading. On the Island, sports enthusiasts tend to go in for a much greater variety of activities than on the mainland and to take part in them for many years, probably longer than in other provinces. Even

In summer, Islanders head for the beach or for the country. While visitors favour the white sand beaches of the north shore, many Islanders prefer southern beaches where bathing is warmer.

allowing for this, the figure shows that sport and recreation are a central feature of Island life.

Largely responsible is a surprising desire for intense competition — at least in the winter months, for in summer there has been a marked trend towards purely recreational exercise. But winter is the season for hockey and curling, both Island favourites, and nowhere in Canada is competitive spirit in these sports stronger.

The Island is probably better equipped for hockey than any other part of North America. There are more than twenty indoor rinks, all well patronized and most of them erected as a result of community fund-raising. In recent years proportionately more professional hockey players have emerged from the Island than from any other province.

In terms of the numbers involved, curling remains second to hockey in popularity, but Island curlers have achieved even more distinction than their hockey counterparts. The sport was introduced to the Island in the 1920s, but not until the 1960s did it emerge as a strong influence. Since then it has expanded rapidly, and in 1977 a rink

Softball is the most popular summer team sport, but it is overshadowed by winter's hockey and curling, which bring out the Islanders' competitive instincts to the full.

Island winters are long and snow lies deep on the ground. Conditions are ideal for snowmobiling and cross-country skiing.

from Charlottetown won the men's junior world championship.

There are many other winter sports on the Island — for instance, figure and speed skating, and ordinary pleasure skating on frozen brooks, streams, and ponds. Skating parties and bonfires are very much part of the snow season. In recent years cross-country skiing has greatly increased in popularity, and there is even some downhill skiing at Brookvale in central Queens.

Summer recreation is quite different. Softball has the most popular competitive support and, if anything, it is even more vocal than on the mainland. Baseball and track and field are prominent too. But in recent years many Islanders have turned to less hectic pursuits — for instance, cycling, lawn bowling, and golf.

Another popular summer activity is fishing, both inland and offshore. Up to 30 per cent of Islanders take part in it one way or another, and of course numbers of tourists as well — particularly in the offshore fishery. Inland, the chief quarries are brook and rainbow trout and Atlantic salmon.

Offshore, chief interest is in the tuna fishery, a recent phenomenon in that it was first organized in 1967. The tuna caught in the Gulf of St. Lawrence are the world's largest bluefins, and big game sports fishermen are drawn to the Island from all parts of the world. The visitors — and Islanders wanting to participate — charter a fishing boat, probably splitting costs among them. All equipment is provided, and the skipper is in charge. The charterers take it in turn to sit in the fighting chair, and when a tuna strikes, remain there until it is lost or brought to gaff.

According to custom, all boated tuna belong to the skipper, though no doubt there will be time for photographs ashore before the fish is despatched to the processing plant. Charters normally set out in the morning and return in the evening, but may stay out long after dark if a tuna is hooked and fighting.

Leafy rural lanes offer fine opportunities for cross-country horseback riding, a favourite leisure pursuit on the Island.

HARNESS RACING

Yet another of the Island's many titles is 'Canada's Kentucky,' a tribute to the excellence of its horses. The horses are Standardbreds, the crucial element in a sport followed by virtually the entire Island community.

The sport of Standardbred harness racing originated on the United States' eastern seaboard during the nineteenth century as an alternative to Thoroughbred flat racing. It began with competition between farmers, then moved on to racetracks in both the United States and Canada. Islanders became involved both as spectators and participants.

At one time there was a network of racetracks covering the Island, but most have been forced out of business by strong competition from the major driving parks of Charlottetown and Summerside. The bigger tracks offer substantial purse money, subsidized by pari mutuel betting, and inevitably they attract the cream of the crop. Races are run all year round at Summerside — twice a week during winter, once a week during summer, but with double cards offered during the Lobster Carnival. Charlotte-

town works towards a peak of five nights of racing each week during July, and during Old Home Week offers fifteen cards in ten days — a North American record.

In fact, both the Lobster Carnival and Old Home Week appear to revolve around harness racing, as if it is the prime reason why Islanders return home each year — which may not be far from the truth. Even Islanders who have no active contact with the sport know many who are involved, and most are familiar with it from childhood.

The most fascinating aspect of Island harness racing is the knowledge displayed by all those associated with it. To the dismay of driving park operators, only a limited proportion of those attending a meeting — probably fewer than two-thirds — actually bet. The others pay the price of administration merely to watch races.

Harness racing is not confined to the Island; it is popular throughout the Maritimes and, of course, beyond. But of some 750 Standardbred breeders and buyers active in the Maritimes, 200 — all breeders — are Islanders. For them, harness racing is a business, and it is the same for the many trainers on the Island.

At any given time, these trainers are responsible for more than 500 horses. Many of the horses are stabled at the tracks in Charlottetown and Summerside, but others are at private tracks across the Island. Inevitably, trainers make money. But for the owners concerned, there is probably only a small return, since most are in racing only for sport.

A high proportion of the owners drive their own horses, sitting on the sulky. If they do not drive themselves, they will probably entrust their horses to a close friend or relative. Some horses may be raced on successive nights, but most trainers prefer their charges to run on only one night in five.

The Island's premier racetrack is the Charlottetown Driving Park, in operation since 1890. During Charlottetown's Old Home Week the track runs fifteen cards in ten days, a North American record. Among the events is the race for the Gold Cup and Saucer, the Island's most prestigious trophy.

Many horses are stabled at the driving parks in Charlottetown and Summerside, but many more are trained on private tracks scattered across the Island. Not for nothing is the Island nicknamed 'Canada's Kentucky.'

During the 1950s, competition became so stiff that many owners took to importing Standardbreds from outside the Maritimes, particularly from Central Canada and the United States. It seemed that the local horse-breeding industry might be eclipsed. In response, breeders introduced the Atlantic Sires Stake Program in 1967.

The program — the first of its kind in Canada — involves the progeny of sires and dams registered in the Maritimes (though the sires and dams might have been introduced from outside). The progeny, fillies and colts bred in the Maritimes, are sold at annual yearling sales organized by the Atlantic Standard Breed Horsebreeders Association.

Registered colts and fillies are eligible for the stakes program. Their owners make regular contributions of stake money to a pool over a period of time until the horses are ready to race. The pool is amplified by contributions from the three Maritime governments, which draw revenue from a tax on bets laid on the pari mutuel.

The horses race in a number of classes, whether they are colts or fillies, trotters or pacers. (Where pacers swing the legs on one side together, trotters co-ordinate diagonal opposites.) Each track in the Maritimes hosts all classes during the year, usually at different meets and combined with events on the normal 'overnight' racing card.

The program has been a great success. Where Island owners used to buy their horses from the United States and Ontario, it is not unlikely that in future, outside buyers will visit the Island.

A blacksmith shoes a horse at the Charlottetown Driving Park. Horses are Standardbreds — not as big as Thoroughbreds, but with longer bodies, heavier limbs, and more stamina.

55

Old-style square dancing remains popular in many parts of the Island, a tradition recalling the bees and frolics of earlier days.

THE ISLANDERS

Significantly, Islanders expressing pride in their home sometimes refer to it as 'My Island' instead of 'Our Island.' The impression is that each feels personal responsibility for its well-being, if not outright proprietorship.

Certainly each inhabitant has very definite views on the Island, or at least on his or her particular community, and often they are strongly opposed to those of neighbours. But paradoxically, outsiders are quickly made aware of a very real Island sense of identity, quite different from anything that springs from the mainland.

The mainland is clearly visible from many points of the south shore. Most Islanders simply call it 'the other side' (of Northumberland Strait). Yet outsiders, even those who have lived on the Island for many years, are dismissed as 'coming from away,' whether from New Brunswick, the Magdalen islands, or Timbuctoo.

In fact, it is said that people cannot be Islanders unless they have had two generations buried there before them. The requirement is not easy to understand, for no special honour is involved. It is simply a matter of acceptance in the Island community as someone who belongs there — and that may be honour enough.

In spite of this carefully maintained pedigree, the Island community is split several ways. The three groups that settled the Island in successive ages are still represented and have kept their cultures alive. There are Micmac Indians and Acadian francophones, as well as anglophones of English, Scottish, and Irish (and even Acadian) descent.

The Micmacs never have been numerous, and today there are fewer than 500 of them. They live in scattered bands, most of them on Lennox Island in Malpeque Bay, which is connected with the Island proper by a causeway. Island Micmacs are famous for the high quality of the baskets they weave from black ash.

The Acadians, too, are mostly located in Prince, where they comprise nearly 25 per cent of the population. They keep a relatively low profile politically and are largely unknown to Islanders farther east, but they have doggedly kept their culture alive and currently it is flourishing.

Island Acadians keep close touch with their counterparts in New Brunswick, but are loyal to their own traditions. They remain close to their churches, and have not undergone the 'Quiet Revolution' which has so changed the situation of francophones in New Brunswick and Quebec. Indeed, although they can receive radio and television programs from Radio-Canada stations on the mainland, they pay little heed to them. It may be that the Acadians are truer 'Islanders' than the anglophones, who have undergone major upheavals in recent times through the introduction of alien influences from outside.

Of course, these influences have long been present. From the Island's beginnings, it was open to outside trade,

Farmers come together at country fairs, which are much like their counterparts of a century ago. This is the annual Crapaud fair, first organized in 1820.

particularly in the mid-nineteenth century. More recently it has received tens of thousands of visitors each year from the United States and Canada, apart from Islanders returning home from self-imposed exile.

The arrival of television, however, has been the great catalyst. Islanders can see what is happening 'away,' and can feel the influence of Toronto in their living rooms. Toronto newspapers are delivered to the Island on the day that they are published. The media encourage Islanders to think of themselves as Canadians, and in the process threaten to weaken their special loyalties to the community.

Old one-room schools and traditional general stores are still to be seen in many parts of the Island. They serve as reminders of the strong rural heritage which is the basis of Island culture.

Acadians

It is supposed that Island Acadians are mostly descended from thirty families of the Malpeque region who took to the woods when those of Port La Joye were expelled by the British in the 1750s. Their community was later expanded by new arrivals from New Brunswick and from the islands of St. Pierre and Miquelon, off Newfoundland.

When Island land lots were first parcelled out, absentee landlords encouraged Acadian families to pioneer settlement and help new arrivals from the British Isles. In many areas the two communities co-existed happily in spite of language difficulties, but in some they did not, and the Acadians were forced out.

As the Island filled with settlers, there was less land available. Acadians were not noted for small families, and

The Rustico region in north-central Queens has always been predominantly Acadian, and cultural traditions run strong. Rustico is now surrounded by anglophone communities, but there are other Acadian settlements in northern, western, and southern Prince, and in eastern Kings.

young couples were hard pressed to make an adequate living. On the initiative of their priests, many left their original communities to open up new settlements in other parts of the Island or even far away from it.

In this way several large parties of Acadians left the Island, particularly during the 1880s. One settled on Cape Breton Island, a second pioneered the Matapedia valley in Quebec, a third settled north of Moncton in New Brunswick. Those who remained on the Island lived by agriculture and fishing, and by their religion.

Regrettably, for a long period Acadians were treated as second-class citizens by their anglophone neighbours. That they have retained their culture is due chiefly to their priests and, in recent times, to the St. Thomas Aquinas Society founded in 1919. They now have their own weekly newspaper and the full support of the Island government.

Beaconsfield in Charlottetown is the headquarters of the P.E.I Heritage Foundation, formed in 1970. The house was built in 1877 by the shipbuilder James Peake.

Elmira station in northern Kings has been restored as an Island railway museum.

At Green Park in northern Prince, the former home of the shipbuilder James Yeo, a shipyard is being recreated to commemorate the days when Island-built ships sailed the Seven Seas.

HERITAGE

Two developments of recent years have underlined Islanders' determination to keep their own identity and resist absorption by the rest of Canada. One has been concern over land ownership, the other growing awareness of their Island heritage.

As regards land, the growth of the tourist industry encouraged outside developers to buy shorefront land on the Island. Residents became increasingly concerned as more changed hands, until in 1972 the province passed legislation which required non-residents to obtain cabinet permission before buying more than four hectares fronting the sea.

The decision was later challenged in the courts by disgruntled Americans, but the Supreme Court of Canada ruled in the Island's favour. Other provinces have since followed the Island's lead, and it is now an established principle that each province has the right to limit non-resident ownership of its territory.

The controversy over land ownership on the Island was paralleled by concern over land use, particularly the decline of agriculture. The province established a Land Use Commission to guide government policy on both questions, and to hear appeals from private citizens unhappy with developments.

The debate over land was a direct continuation of the age-old battle against absentee landlords, which has underlain all Island history. The movement to preserve its heritage, however, is relatively new. Earlier generations were by definition isolated, and had no choice but to live within their heritage.

As communications with the rest of Canada have improved, however, that situation has changed. Outside interests might quickly submerge pride in the Island's past if not deliberately counteracted. In 1970 the province established the Prince Edward Island Heritage Foundation to conserve and restore the Island's historic resources.

As its headquarters, the foundation acquired Beaconsfield, a mansion in Charlottetown originally built by a wealthy shipbuilder in 1877. It houses a growing collection of Islandiana donated to, or purchased by, the foundation, which organizes exhibitions dealing with Island themes.

Beaconsfield was purchased with part of a one-million-dollar 'birthday gift' to the Island from the federal government to mark its centennial in Confederation, celebrated in 1973. For a time there was fierce debate on whether it should be spent on new sports facilities or on heritage preservation, but heritage won.

It was suggested — not altogether flippantly — that the whole Island should be preserved in a time capsule. This was obviously impractical, but the Heritage Foundation went some way towards realizing the ideal by selecting typical sites scattered throughout the Island to illustrate particular facets of the past.

One was Orwell Corner, a well-preserved country crossroads in eastern Queens. In earlier days such crossroads were the focal points of the surrounding rural community. Today Orwell Corner is being revitalized. Most of its buildings now belong to the foundation and are open to the public each summer. They include a store, a working farm, and a school. The church, though no longer in use, still belongs to the United Church. Further buildings, including a community hall, a blacksmith's shop, and a shingle mill will be added.

A second heritage complex repre-sents the fishing industry. It has been established at Basin Head on the eastern coast. Reconstructed fishing shacks are grouped at a small cove among dunes, near an old canning plant. In addition there is an interpretive centre housing displays and illustrating local ecology.

Green Park in north-eastern Prince near Bideford, originally the home of the merchant and shipbuilder James Yeo, Jr. has been restored and furnished to the tastes of 1865. A working shipyard is being established on the creek from which many of Yeo's ships were launched. There is an interpretive centre there too.

These three monuments to Island heritage were developed through the centennial gift, as was a stand of climax forest near Souris. The foundation has since cast its net wider. Elmira station in northern Kings, acquired from Canadian National, has been turned into a railway museum.

Orwell Corner, made famous through the writings of Sir Andrew Macphail, is a rural crossroads which was originally the social and economic focus of the surrounding farming community. A church, school, and general store have survived, and a community hall destroyed by fire some years ago is to be recreated.

ENVIRONMENT

Concern for the environment has affected all Canada, and the Island no less than elsewhere. But while other regions have been plagued by pollution of air and water, on the Island the chief menace has been pollution of the landscape.

Former generations seem to have produced little waste and, consequently, little land pollution. Their chief problem was removal of eyesores like tumbledown buildings and overgrown land lots. The traditions of those days linger in the annual awards of the Island Rural Beautification Society.

With the arrival of the 'throwaway society,' however, the Island suddenly faced problems — especially serious in a province whose face is its fortune. More than 300 unofficial open garbage dumps appeared across the Island, as well as thousands of derelict cars. These vehicles were abandoned to rust at the roadside or wherever their owners left them. Their proliferation greatly upset the various communities, and the first big effort of the Department of the Environment, set up by the Island gov-

ernment, was to salvage the rusting bodies and send them for crushing.

In the course of two years some 20 000 vehicles were collected in this way, and the problem has been solved. Besides, a number of large refuse containers placed strategically has helped clear up the rest of the garbage menace. In addition the government has passed legislation discouraging the use of throwaway bottles and cans.

But that is only a beginning. Another form of landscape pollution has been the placing of large advertising billboards along the highways, both a distraction for motorists and unfair competition for the landscape. Again these were offensive to Islanders and visitors, and they have been outlawed.

There is a program in operation to clear up disused shale pits, and besides this, a ban on removing sand from dunes or beaches without permission. This is partly for aesthetic reasons and partly to prevent the breaking-up of dunes and the consequent inundation of agricultural land or the silting up of fishing harbours by loose sand.

Concern for the environment clearly precludes the introduction of industries

When disturbed, sand dunes of the north and west coasts threaten to inundate agricultural land and to silt up fishing harbours. Sand may not be removed from the dunes without government permission, and visitors and Islanders are discouraged from trampling the plant growth on the dunes since the plants prevent the sand from spreading.

likely to pollute air or water, and the Island will stay clean. In addition, many Islanders now want to prevent the introduction of 'progressive' projects which may be out of keeping with Island tradition. A case in point was a 'medieval castle' planned for the Cavendish area as a tourist attraction. Debate on whether construction should be allowed to proceed came to involve the whole Island community, and was eventually the subject of public hearings before the Land Use Commission.

A series of scale models of famous castles and other buildings in Europe was already in existence near by — the Woodleigh Replicas, which have become one of the Island's leading attractions. They had sprung from the hobby of an Island resident, so they could be

Parks and Wildlife

Besides its national park, the Island has nearly forty provincial parks, offering a wide variety of experiences. Most are purely recreational, but a growing number cater to the nature lover and the wilderness seeker. One wilderness park is that named after Sir Andrew Macphail, near Orwell Corner in Kings, and two more are being developed.

As regards wildlife, the Island has long since lost all traces of the big game once in occupation — moose and black bear. The most important surviving mammal is the red fox, which is in no danger of extinction because it breeds prolifically. Even so, its numbers have been greatly reduced through trapping.

Other mammals are trapped, including the beaver, muskrat, raccoon, and skunk. Today's beavers are the descendants of stock introduced from the mainland after the original Island beaver population died out. Skunks and raccoons were originally introduced in the 1900s and were farmed for their pelts.

When the value of the pelts decreased, fur ranchers released the animals and they ran wild. Their descendants have become part of the natural environment, along with 'authentic' members like the snow hare, red squirrel, mink, and ermine. There is also rich bird life, including several species of birds of prey, great blue herons, and the Island's provincial bird, the blue jay.

The Island's most distinctive surviving mammal is the red fox, which is trapped extensively but is in no danger of extinction.

Tidy landscapes are an Island tradition of long standing, but for a time the 'throwaway society' threatened to get the better of them. A continuing battle against land pollution keeps the menace at bay.

said to be an authentic feature of Island life.

The Cavendish castle, on the other hand, was deliberately exotic and could be regarded as a potential precedent for many similar ventures. Islanders dug in their heels to resist, remembering a number of ill-fated tourists traps of the 1960s which linger as decaying eyesores, polluting the landscape.

The traditionalists lost their battle, but in the process raised interesting questions that underlined the difficulty facing the Island's Department of Tourism. Its job is to balance the value of job creation through the tourist industry against the cost of affecting the Island environment. So far all is well, but it must maintain vigilant guard.

In the course of two years the provincial government's Department of the Environment collected 20 000 abandoned vehicles and sent them for crushing. The campaign eliminated a major pollution problem.

GREEN GABLES

Mark Twain considered Anne of Green Gables to be 'the dearest, most moving and delightful child since the immortal Alice,' and each year droves of visitors happily scour the Island for locations described in Lucy Maud Montgomery's books.

Most attention is directed to the Cavendish region, where Anne the orphan was taken in by Marilla and Matthew Cuthbert and Lucy Maud herself was raised by her grandparents following the early death of her mother.

Much later in life, Lucy Maud Montgomery admitted that the house she described as the Cuthbert home was an amalgam of several she had known in the Cavendish valley. Another, very like Lucy Maud's grandparents' home, has now been converted into the Green Gables post office. The original home, which had accommodated a small post office in its front parlour, burned down years ago.

This house in Clifton, near New London, was Lucy Maud Montgomery's birthplace. Her mother died when she was two, and when her father moved to Saskatchewan, she went to live with her grandparents in Cavendish.

Visitors are drawn from all over the world, but particularly from Japan where *Anne of Green Gables* is required reading in the school curriculum. In 1976 a young Japanese couple travelled to Cavendish to be married in the church on the hill where 'Anne' had played the organ.

Lucy Maud Montgomery wrote the first three Anne books while living in Cavendish and helping her grandmother in the post office. After her marriage in

The Cavendish house preserved as 'Green Gables' was the home of the cousins of Lucy Maud Montgomery. The house's rooms correspond to those described in the Anne novels, with three upstairs bedrooms, a parlour, a dining room, and a large kitchen.

1911 she spent most of the rest of her life in Ontario. But on her death in 1942, her body was buried in Cavendish cemetery.

62

Photograph Credits

Humphry Clinker: p. 14 centre left, p. 45 top, and bottom right, p. 52 bottom left, p. 54, p. 58 top; *Environment Canada*: p. 31 bottom, (Leo Cave) p. 3 bottom; *Fisheries Canada*: p. 32 top, p. 33 top, p. 35 top; *Industrial Enterprise Inc.*: p. 23 top right, p. 35 bottom; *Island Information Service*: p. 23 top left and bottom, p. 25 top and centre, p. 26 top and bottom, p. 27 top and bottom, p. 29, p. 30 top and bottom, p. 33 bottom, p. 39 top, p. 41 top, p. 44, p. 45 bottom centre, p. 46 top, p. 48, p. 49 centre, p. 58 bottom right, p. 61 centre; *Maritime Electric Co.*: p. 40, p. 41 bottom left and right; *National Air Photo Library*: p. 4 top; *Prince Edward Island Dept. of Education*: p. 49 top and bottom; *Prince Edward Island Dept. of Tourism, Parks and Conservation*: p. 5. top, and bottom left and right, p. 6, p. 7 top and bottom, p. 8 left and top and bottom right, p. 11 bottom, p. 16, p. 18 bottom, p. 22, p. 24, p. 25 bottom, p. 28, p. 31 top, p. 32 bottom, p. 34, p. 36 top, and bottom left and right, p. 37, p. 38 top and bottom, p. 39 bottom, p. 42 top and bottom, p. 43 top, p. 46 bottom, p. 47, p. 51 bottom, p. 52 top and bottom right, p. 53, p. 55 top and bottom, p. 56 top and bottom, p. 57 top and bottom, p. 58 bottom left, p. 59, p. 60, p. 61 top and centre, p. 62 top and bottom; *Public Archives of Prince Edward Island*: p. 8 top right, p. 9, p. 10 top, p. 11 top, p. 12 top, p. 13 bottom, p. 14 centre right and centre left, p. 20 bottom, p. 45 bottom left and right, p. 50 centre.

Acknowledgments

Many individuals, corporations, institutions, and government departments assisted us in gathering information and illustrations. Among them we owe special thanks to the following:

Francis Blanchard
CN Marine
Charlottetown Chamber of Commerce
Charlottetown Driving Park
Confederation Centre of the Arts
Environment Canada
Fisheries Canada
Jacques Gaudereau
Industrial Enterprises Incorporated
Institute of Man and Resources
The Island
Island Information Service
C. M. MacLean Limited

Maritime Electric Company
Prince Edward Island Department of Agriculture and Forestry
Prince Edward Island Department of Development
Prince Edward Island Department of Education
Prince Edward Island Department of the Environment
Prince Edward Island Department of Fisheries
Prince Edward Island Department of Health
Prince Edward Island Department of Industry and Commerce
Prince Edward Island Department of Justice and the Attorney-General
Prince Edward Island Department of Municipal Affairs

Prince Edward Island Department of Social Services
Prince Edward Island Department of Tourism, Parks and Conservation
Prince Edward Island Federation of Agriculture
Prince Edward Island Heritage Foundation
Prince Edward Island Hospital Services
Prince Edward Island Land Use Commission
Prince Edward Island Marketing Board
Prince Edward Island Potato Marketing Board
Public Archives of Prince Edward Island
Ed Watters

If we have unwittingly infringed copyright in any photograph reproduced in this publication, we tender our sincere apologies and will be glad of the opportunity, upon being satisfied as to the owner's title, to pay an appropriate fee as if we had been able to obtain prior permission.

Canadian Cataloguing in Publication Data

Hocking, Anthony, 1944-
    Prince Edward Island

(Canada series)

Includes index.
ISBN 0-07-082683-8

1. Prince Edward Island. 2. Prince Edward Island—Description and travel. I. Series.

FC2611.6.H63   971.7   C77-001601-4
F1047.5.H63

1 2 3 4 5 6 7 8 9 0 BP 7 6 5 4 3 2 1 9 8

Printed and bound in Canada

Index

CANADIAN STATISTICS

	Joined Confed-eration	Capital	Area	Population (1976)	Ethnic Origin (% 1971)		
					British	French	Other
CANADA		Ottawa	9 976 185 km²	22 992 604	45	29	26
Newfoundland	1949	St. John's	404 519 km²	557 725	94	3	3
Prince Edward Island	1873	Charlottetown	5 657 km²	118 229	83	14	3
Nova Scotia	1867	Halifax	55 491 km²	828 571	77	10	13
New Brunswick	1867	Fredericton	74 437 km²	677 250	58	37	5
Quebec	1867	Quebec City	1 540 687 km²	6 234 445	11	79	10
Ontario	1867	Toronto	1 068 587 km²	8 264 465	59	10	31
Manitoba	1870	Winnipeg	650 090 km²	1 021 506	42	9	49
Saskatchewan	1905	Regina	651 903 km²	921 323	42	6	52
Alberta	1905	Edmonton	661 188 km²	1 838 037	47	6	47
British Columbia	1871	Victoria	948 600 km²	2 466 608	58	4	38
Yukon	—	Whitehorse	536 327 km²	21 836	49	7	56
Northwest Territories	—	Yellowknife	3 379 699 km²	42 609	25	7	68